Responding to the culture of death

A primer of bioethical issues

John R Ling

© Day One Publications 2001
First printed 2001

All Scripture quotations are taken from The New International Version.© 1973, 1978,
1984, International Bible Society. Published by Hodder and Stoughton.

British Library Cataloguing in Publication Data available
ISBN 1 903087 26-0

Published by Day One Publications
Ryelands Road, Leominster, HR6 8NZ, England
TEL 01568 613 740 FAX 01568 611 473
email—sales@dayone.co.uk
www.dayone.co.uk

Designed by Steve Devane and printed by Orchard Press (Cheltenham) Ltd.

For Wendy

Contents

Acknowledgements

As the author, of course, I must take responsibility for the conception of this little primer, but there are many others who have helped me greatly during the time of its gestation and birth.

First, there were those men who informed and shaped my early thinking about bioethical issues. Above all, there were the late Francis Schaeffer and C Everett Koop, who, with their project, *Whatever Happened to the Human Race?*, opened my eyes to the issues of abortion, infanticide, and euthanasia in the late 1970s. Second, there have been many friends and co-labourers within LIFE, the UK's leading pro-life charity, especially Jack and Nuala Scarisbrick, who have been, and remain, shining examples of people who respond, not only by speaking out against such horrors, but by actually doing something positive to resist and overcome them. Third, there have been those good Christian men and women who contributed to the success and influence of Evangelicals for LIFE, a specialist grouping within the LIFE organization. Fourth, there have been my opponents; some ranting feminists, a few thoughtful students, and a handful of sceptical Christians, who have made me think harder and longer about these bioethical issues. Finally, there is my wife, Wendy, who has been a real helpmeet and encourager in this work—without her, this book would never have been completed.

'One of the surest characteristics of a civilised society is its respect for the sanctity of human life. Indeed, life in all its forms demands our respect, but it is human life in particular whose sanctity we affirm, because it is the life of persons made in the image of God (Genesis 9:6).

'By this criterion our country has for twenty years steadily been slipping back into barbarism. For the abortion statistics are truly horrifying, and the framers of the 1967 Abortion Act never intended, or even anticipated that it would permit the slaughter of nearly three million unborn children. No, the Act has been seriously—even flagrantly—abused. In consequence, morally-sensitive people will not rest until it has been repealed and its provisions tightened. Nor can we come to terms with any legislation which tolerates experimentation on the living human embryo.

'Moreover, the sanctity of human life extends beyond the foetus to the well-being of the mother, of the family and of the child after birth. I am thankful that LIFE cherishes this holistic vision. We are anti-abortion and anti-experimentation because we are pro-life. We need to be consistent in the seeking to protect human life at every stage in its journey from the womb to the tomb.'

Rev. Dr John RW Stott, (1987) *Evangelicals for LIFE Newsletter.*

'But it is an appalling thought that in the present state of this country and its morals—the whole condition of society—somehow or other *we* are failing. When we contrast ourselves with what our forefathers did in such times, I think we should put on sackcloth and ashes and feel utterly ashamed of ourselves. We seem to be living in our 'cieled houses' and to be ready to believe that everything is all right as long as everything is all right with us. The whole general situation seems to pass by default as far as we are concerned.'

'Now I think that one can justify movements and societies for the purpose of taking action of a social or a semi-political nature. Here you are not in

Quotations

the realm of doctrine but you are confronted by practical circumstances in which certain things need to be done ... I do not think that there is any difficulty about justifying that.'

Dr Martyn Lloyd-Jones, (1989) *Knowing The Times,* Banner of Truth Trust.

'If the Church of Jesus Christ, or indeed the individual Christian, ceases to proclaim God's righteous standards and the inevitable ruin which follows upon disobedience, we are being cruel and unloving to our fellow human beings. They may look at us one day and say: "You *knew*, and you didn't warn us!" We will have been guilty of not blowing the trumpet.'

Raymond Johnston, (1990) *Caring and Campaigning,* Marshall Pickering.

'If you falter in times of trouble,
  how small is your strength!
Rescue those being led away to death;
  hold back those staggering towards slaughter.
If you say, "But we knew nothing about this,"
  does not he who weighs the heart perceive it?
Does not he who guards your life know it?
Will he not repay each person according to what he has done?'

PROVERBS 24:10-12.

How I came to respond

When it comes to bioethics, I was a late-starter. Somehow or other, the debate surrounding the 1967 Abortion Act passed me by, even though at the time I was a student at that hotbed of radical student politics, Leeds University. I should have known better. Instead, my bioethical wake-up call probably came in 1971, while I was studying at the Pennsylvania State University. One Sunday a preacher at the church I attended held up a copy of *Life* magazine and showed the amazing photographs, taken by Lennart Nilsson, of the developing unborn child. 'Look', he said, 'See how wonderfully you and I have been formed in the womb. Yet some people want to kill such exquisite life.' It was my introduction to the issue of abortion, though I was largely unmoved.

Yes, I was a late-starter, and I was also a late-developer. It took almost another ten years before I was again challenged by the subject of abortion. This time it was coupled with the issues of infanticide and euthanasia in the films associated with the *Whatever Happened to the Human Race?* project of the late Francis Schaeffer and C Everett Koop. This time the bioethical penny dropped. Two years later I became the founding chairman of the Aberystwyth LIFE Group, co-founder of Evangelicals for LIFE, and the regional representative for Wales on the Central Committee of the LIFE organization—my life was never to be the same again!

Since that time I have spoken on many of these bioethical issues at public, church, school, university, and women's meetings throughout the UK. I have also addressed similar gatherings in Denmark, Germany, Holland, and Latvia. In addition, I have written numerous articles on subjects such as abortion, in vitro fertilization, genetics, surrogacy, and euthanasia for a range of newspapers and magazines, both Christian and secular. I have been invited to broadcast several times on radio and television. I have also been a 'foot soldier' and organized fund-raising events, mail-shots, leaflet deliveries, petitions, and so on. And for the last ten years I have taught a course, entitled Bioethical Issues, for undergraduate students at the University of Wales, Aberystwyth.

These are my pro-life credentials. Yet they are a catalogue of almost 'too little, too late'. In that respect I am not unlike most other evangelical

Christians, but that is no excuse. Almost all of us have been bioethical 'Johnny-come-latelies'. But how could this be? How could an educated, family man, who reads newspapers, watches television, and has easy access to the best libraries and other information systems throughout the world, be unaware of, and unmoved by, these issues that are directly affecting many of the people around him? I do not know the answer, but I sometimes ask myself the question.

The culture of death

Twenty years ago, when I first responded, it was all so much simpler. By and large, there was then only one issue, abortion. To that can now be added the complexities of infanticide, surrogacy, in vitro fertilization, human embryo experimentation, genetic engineering, euthanasia, prenatal screening, eugenics, contraception, gene therapy, infertility, cloning, persistent vegetative state, foetal pain, and several others.

This is a sad, sad list of medical endeavour. Over each of these topics there is the pall, or smell, of death because practically all of them result, directly or indirectly, in the death of human beings. They are examples of a perverse and inhumane medicine, a medicine that has gone wrong. This is a medicine that has its roots in secular humanism and the fruits it produces are horrible. Indeed, they constitute a culture of death. Of course, not all medicine has become so corrupted or tainted. But make no mistake, this culture of death is the very warp and weft of much of modern medicine, and it has infected us all.

The purpose of this book

Negatives can sometimes help define the positives. This book is *not* an academic book. It does not get bogged down with scores of obscure references and tedious footnotes, but that does not mean it is a book for the unthinking. This book is *not* a theoretical book. It does not dissect the minutiae of sterile bioethical ideologies, but rather it is a practical workbook. This book is *not* a comprehensive book. It does not encompass every bioethical topic, but it does deal with some of the key issues and some crucial statements. Prominent among these are the issue of abortion and the statements of the Warnock Report. So this book is a taster of bioethics, a mere primer, yet also a principled manual.

When I have presented any of these bioethical issues to Christian audiences, two particular topics tend to generate the greatest interest. One is exploring what the Bible has to say, and the other is answering the question, So what can we do? This primer, above all, rehearses these two topics. Apart from the chapter that surveys 'Some of the primary issues', these topics occupy the two largest chapters of the book. And that is how I always wanted it to be. It is the great Christian interlock—the exposition of Scripture, followed by the application of Scripture. I am still convinced, as was my experience in the late 1970s, that when a Christian understands, or 'sees', these bioethical issues in the light of Scripture, then that all-important question will inevitably be asked, and earnestly so.

Therefore the aims of this book are rather simple, and two-fold. First, it is to provide Christians with the biblical basis for understanding past, current, and future bioethical issues, especially within this area of human medicine. It is for those Christians, who, in their heart-of-hearts, know that they should be against abortion, surrogacy, human embryo experimentation, euthanasia, and the like, but are not quite sure why. They have never seriously thought through these issues. So, if that is your position, then this book was certainly written with you in mind. But it is not intended as a primer only for armchair casuistry. Biblical Christianity demands that its doctrines affect our lives, and radically so. This is the book's second aim. It wants you out of your armchair and doing. It wants you to respond. It wants to change how you think, speak, and act about these bioethical issues. This is what nowadays we might call 'joined-up Christianity'.

John R Ling
Aberystwyth
January 2001

Chapter 1

Introduction

1.1 The origins of the culture of life

It is often said that Western human medicine has a long and illustrious history. Its origins lie in a combination of the pagan Hippocratic oath and the Christian doctrines. For well over 2,000 years, these two grand pillars have underpinned both medical ethics and medical practice. Their influence for good can be demonstrated by, for example, the enduring Hippocratic phrase, 'Do no patient any harm', and what has become known as the Christian golden rule as spelled out in Matthew 7:12, but earlier, and more succinctly as, 'Love your neighbour as yourself' (Leviticus 19:18; Matthew 22:39). These two great maxims, together with other of the Hippocratic and Christian precepts, have provided practitioners of medicine with a powerful restraint, as well as a positive motivation, and it is these which have kept medicine largely safe and wholesome for centuries.

Medicine was, from its earliest times, regarded as the healing art. The doctor's duty was to care for, and to treat, and, if possible, to cure the patient. In short, good medicine was an integral part of a culture of life. Sickness and disease were regarded as medicine's constant enemies, although the inevitability of natural death was well understood and accepted. But unnatural death was something else. Any doctor who caused it was a renegade—deliberately killing patients was never a part of proper medicine. Indeed, the Hippocratic oath specifically forbade both euthanasia and abortion: 'I will give no deadly drug to any, though it be asked of me, nor will I counsel such, and especially I will not aid a woman to procure abortion.' Such practices were regarded as bad medicine and therefore anathema to the culture of life.

And for two millennia, medicine did, on the whole, uphold this culture of life. The progress of medicine has been spectacular and we have all benefited from its surgery, drugs, vaccinations, and so on. The average life expectancy in Britain at the beginning of the last century was a mere forty-nine years for men and fifty-two for women, now it stands at seventy-five and eighty, respectively. Today our lives are, in many ways, significantly easier than those of our forefathers, primarily because of the application of good medicine. Its culture of life has undeniably brought health and happiness. For this we should be thankful.

1.2 The origins of the culture of death

So we may ask: Where did modern medicine go wrong? How did we lose this wonderful culture of life, and gain this ugly culture of death?

Medicine's own guiding principles, its own 'confessions of faith', demonstrate just how recently it has become corrupted. Initially, as we have seen, the Hippocratic oath took an uncompromising stance against abortion and euthanasia and insisted that doctors, 'Do no patient any harm'. Over the intervening 2,000 years other oaths, or declarations, concerning medical ethics and practice have echoed this Hippocratic oath. For example, the Declaration of Geneva (adopted by the General Assembly of the World Medical Organization in 1948) stated, 'I will maintain the utmost respect for human life from the time of conception, even under threat I will not use my medical knowledge contrary to the laws of humanity.' That was written just two generations ago.

But more recent revisions have been much weaker affairs. They have reflected the great shift in society as a whole, but in bioethical issues in particular, away from this culture of life. For example, in 1997, the British Medical Association produced a draft revision of the Hippocratic oath. It stated, 'I recognize the special value of human life but I also know that the prolongation of human life is not the only aim of health care. Where abortion is permitted, I agree that it should take place only within an ethical and legal framework.'

Can you see the downgrade? For 2,000 and more years medicine had a high view of human life. Human life was described by adjectives like, special, sacred, and worthy. Within the last fifty or so years medicine has adopted a low view of human life. Now human life is generally considered to be cheap, exploitable, and expendable. This is the culture of death.

These changes, at the very heart of medical ethics and practice, have been alarmingly rapid. Indeed, just about all aspects of our society, be they education, welfare, science, law, economics, whatever, have similarly changed. In truth, we have become dominated by secular humanism. This worldview can be defined as 'man, the measure of all things'. Man, and not God, is now the centre of all things. Man, and not God, is now the law-giver and the judge. Ethics are now man-centred and arbitrary, rather than God-centred and absolute. Practice is now utilitarian, rather than principled. This is the prevailing mindset of our society—and in medicine it has encouraged the spread of the culture of death.

Now modern medicine operates firmly within this culture of death. For example, although abortion has been practised throughout the ages, it was never regarded as proper medicine; it was unlawful, it was done in secret, it was performed by quacks and charlatans. Nowadays, it is generally lawful, widely advertised, and openly practised by untold thousands of highly-qualified doctors, world-wide. In England, Wales, and Scotland abortion was legalized in 1967 and its free supply since then has resulted in the deaths of an estimated 5 million unborn children. Abortion now occurs every day, in the hospitals of every health authority and in the private clinics of every city, wherever we live. This is part of the culture of death.

For the last forty or so years our medical services have developed sophisticated programmes of prenatal screening to search out the unborn who are disabled. Once detected, they are commonly destroyed before birth. Can you comprehend it—doctors prescribing death as a treatment? This is the modern-day practice of eugenics, and it is part of the culture of death.

When the low-weight and the 'unthrifty' are born there is an increasing tendency to let them die. Some hospitals make no caring efforts with babies born below a certain weight. Disabled neonates often suffer the same regimen. After all, we already kill the disabled in utero, so why not kill the disabled newborn, those who have slipped through the prenatal screening net? This is infanticide, and it is part of the culture of death.

In 1990, the UK Parliament sanctioned the use of human embryos for infertility treatments and for destructive experimentation. As a result, thousands and thousands of human embryos have been, and are still being, routinely destroyed. This is part of the culture of death.

For much of the last century there have been repeated attempts to legalize euthanasia. So far these calls have been resisted in the UK, but for how much longer? Other countries are already covertly practising euthanasia; thousands of their elderly and senile are deliberately killed each year. In the UK some hospital patients are already dying because they are denied food and drink, a course of action, which, we are assured, is 'in their best interests'. This too is part of the culture of death.

And these are not just issues for the practitioners of medicine and science, something that goes on behind closed hospital and laboratory doors. These bioethical issues have spilled out of the hospital wards, private clinics, and research centres into our homes, workplaces, and churches. They have affected us all.

We live in a culture of death. How else can you explain that a sophisticated, prosperous, and educated society deliberately puts to death its own offspring, its smallest, its weakest, and its most vulnerable members? We really do live in a culture of death.

So, what can we do about it? How can we respond to it? To start with, we need to apply our minds, to grapple with these issues and come to some understanding of them. And so the first stop for the Christian is the Bible. What does it have to say? How can its teachings marshal our thinking, season our speech, and galvanize our actions?

Themes from the Scriptures

T he firmest foundations for an understanding of bioethical issues come from four major themes from the Scriptures. I like to think of them as the four legs that support a platform. And this biblical platform is unshakeably solid. This biblical platform is one upon which you can stand firm and not be shy, or apologetic. It is not like the wobbly, do-it-yourself botch produced by secular humanism, with its utilitarian thinking, its uncertain declarations, and its arbitrary decisions. Once grasped, these themes from the Scriptures will provide you with not only robust answers, but also the basis for profound understanding and perceptive judgements of all bioethical issues, whether past, present, or future. These themes are the foundations upon which a proper and lasting bioethical superstructure can be safely built—the issues may change, but these themes from the Scriptures are everlastingly durable.

It is so easy, often far too easy for us, to drift along with the flow of this world, to offer no critique of its thinking and no resistance to its practices. Yet every Christian is called to stand up for truth and to resist evil (Ephesians 6:10-20). Christians should therefore often find themselves swimming, or even struggling, against the tide, and that can be difficult. It therefore behoves us to get all the assistance we can. The Bible, as it says of itself, '... is God-breathed and is useful for teaching, rebuking, correcting and training in righteousness, so that the man of God may be thoroughly equipped for every good work' (2 Timothy 3:16-17). Here then is the assistance we need, here then are these four themes from the Scriptures. They are presented here briefly, certainly not comprehensively, but hopefully comprehensibly. So, let's get 'thoroughly equipped'!

2.1 Human life is unique and special

What better place to start than the first book of the Bible, its first chapter, and even its first verse? The Scriptures begin here by telling us that God created everything. God's creative attributes can perhaps best be discerned by examining the Hebrew word *bara*, which means 'created'. It occurs at three key points in the unfolding of creation.

First, it occurs in Genesis 1:1. 'In the beginning God created the heavens and the earth.' Here is the unadorned affirmation that God created something out of nothing, that is, *ex nihilo*. This must be one of the most trenchant sentences in the whole Bible. It is so uncluttered, yet it is so majestic. Look up into a clear night sky and be amazed! Watch a sunset over the sea and be awe-struck! Let your doxology flow! He created it all!

The second time the word occurs is in Genesis 1:21. 'So God created the great creatures of the sea and every living and moving thing with which the water teems, according to their kinds, and every winged bird according to its kind.' Here, (and together with verse 24) God creates conscious life; the fish of the sea, the birds of the air, the animals of the land.

The third occasion on which the word *bara* is used is in Genesis 1:27. 'So God created man in his own image, in the image of God he created him; male and female he created them.' The preceding statement, in verse 26, signifies a notable change; previously God simply spoke and it was, that is, he 'commanded' creation, by his fiat. Now here it becomes, 'Let us...', that is, the Father enters into 'consultation' with the other persons of the Godhead before he creates man and woman. In addition, the three-fold repetition of *bara* in this verse adds force. It is as if the Triune God calls out to us, 'Attention! Listen! This is very important!' Genesis 1:27 is about to become our bioethical cornerstone, *sine qua non*, the very heart of the matter. Capture its significance and we touch transcendence.

Here then is the opening chapter of the Bible. The Creator's overall assessment was: 'God saw all that he had made, and it was very good' (Genesis 1:31). This is the beginning of the culture of life, and in particular, human life—it was good, no, it was '... very good'. This opening chapter is an account in three stages; the creation of the inanimate, the creation of conscious life, the creation of man. So early in Genesis, and then throughout the rest of the Book, there is this clear distinction between man (and, of course, in the generic sense, woman too), and the rest of creation. The Bible maintains that human life is the pinnacle of God's creative endeavours, or what John Calvin, in his commentary, *Genesis* (Banner of Truth, 1965), calls (p. 91) '... the most excellent of all His works ...' and (p. 92) '... something great and wonderful.'

The Bible therefore insists that men and women are different from all other forms of life. We are unique and we are special. Why? Because we are made in the image of God, in the likeness of Deity. We all bear the *imago Dei*. This attribute was given to no other. This is the basis of the dignity of all human beings, it is the ground of our worth. Human beings, men, women, and children, are not nothing. All are intrinsically worthy of the highest respect, as distinct from simple affection. Why? Because we, that is, you, me, and our neighbours, are made in the image of God. Yes, let us say it again: we are unique and we are special. This is good news for the best of days, and for the worst of days.

This astonishing truth can also be captured from quite different angles. Consider the value and worth of a human being from, for example, the perspective of the great biblical theme of redemption. Redemption is God's determination, starting in Genesis 3, to bring men and women back to himself, even after they have resolutely rejected him. Why does he bother? Why does he care? Primarily, because we are made in his image, because we belong to God. That is why he has determined to rescue not poppies, or parrots, or pigs, but only us, only those made in his image. That is a measure of how valuable we are. We all bear this ancient, creational worth (in the sense that Adam was our progenitor), as well as a modern-day, procreational worth (in the sense that we are all participants in the Adamic heritage), which are both God-given and eternal.

These propositions from Genesis are of crucial importance in understanding who we are, and in assessing our value and worth. But these creational doctrines are not addressed to Christians alone. These are truths for all. It makes no difference whether you are a believer, or an unbeliever, because these words have ramifications for the whole of the human race. If these great biblical truths are ignored, denied, or thrown out of the window, what is left? Then what is man or woman? Then we are just cogs in a mechanistic universe, or products of time and chance, in a Godless, impersonal world. These are the very conclusions of modern man about himself—read, for example, the works of Jean-Paul Sartre and Jacques Monod, who were among the leading literary and scientific proponents of this bleak worldview during the last century.

This is all fascinating stuff, but it is no mere fancy philosophy—it affects us all, deeply. You see, the way a man views human life determines how he thinks about, and acts towards, himself, and by implication, towards the rest of the human race too. And this modern thinking, this unbiblical worldview, has produced a low view of human life, in both thought and practice. One must say logically, of course it has, because if you and I are not special, then the door is open to any practice, any abuse. Our society has rejected the biblical view of man. So why are we surprised that infanticide, euthanasia, human embryo destruction, abortion, child sex abuse, pornography, violence and evil of all kinds are so widespread? What else should we expect? Pushed to its ultimate conclusion, such a worldview cannot make a distinction between kicking a chair and kicking a child. After all, both are only collections of molecules containing mostly carbon, oxygen, hydrogen, and nitrogen atoms, aren't they? This is the low view of human life in action. It inevitably results in a culture of death.

In total contrast, the Bible's view of man, as made in the image of God, produces a high view of human life. All human life is therefore precious. All human life is inviolable. All human life is to be respected, protected, defended, and cherished. This will inevitably result in a culture of life. And these two opposing worldviews bear totally different fruits—one is good and beautiful, the other is bad and ugly.

We must understand all this with crystal clarity. Man, made in the image of God, must be foundational to our thinking. If we get this wrong, then everything else that follows will also be wrong. It is like buttoning up a shirt—if one button goes into the wrong buttonhole, everything that follows will be out of kilter. Carrying on is useless, because it will never come right. The way forward is to unbutton the lot, go back to square one, and start again. Go back therefore to Genesis 1.

2.2 Human life begins at conception

The most persistent question in bioethical discussions is this: When does human life begin? Underlying this apparently straightforward and seemingly innocuous question are much more sinister ones such as, can we destructively experiment on human embryos, and when should human life be protected by law, and can we intentionally end early human life by abortion?

So, the original question twists and turns and takes various forms, such as, what, or who, is the unborn? When does 'it' begin, and what is 'its' nature? Is it human, is it a child, is it 'one of us'? Some say, that an embryo, and for that matter a foetus too, is inhuman, though they concede that somehow it is 'becoming' human. Others maintain that it is only a piece of tissue, or a collection of undifferentiated cells. Some say, it is a 'potential' human being. Others say that sentience, that is, when the pre-born can interact with their environment, is the defining characteristic of the start of human life. Others say that viability, when the child can live outside the womb, is the test of real, human existence.

These woolly statements fly in the face of truth, both biblical and scientific. But why would apparently intelligent people ever hold such opinions in the first place? The truth is that they have an ulterior motive. They want to retain the option, and the power, to destroy human embryos, or to eliminate unborn children. These false views therefore allow them to evade the reality of their actions. They can then say, 'It was never a real baby, it was just a little something and nothing.' This is what the culture of death does; it bends the truth and it encourages people to deceive themselves.

One such deceived person was Naomi Wolf, one of the darlings of the US feminist movement, who had long been a leading supporter of abortion-on-demand. She would rally the sisterhood in chanting their platitudes such as, 'a foetus is nothing, a foetus is nothing'. Then in 1994, she became pregnant and, in the midst of morning sickness, she came to the realization that this slogan was a lie and that another adage, 'abortion stops a beating heart' was incontrovertibly true. Her unthinking rhetoric had collapsed in the face of reality—she could evade it no more.

Another prime example of this wayward type of thinking is found in the Warnock Report (1984), which is discussed more fully in later chapters. This Report was the most important and influential document on bioethical issues to be published in the last century. And even today it remains the touchstone for much of modern-day bioethical thinking. Faced with the big question, it unhelpfully concluded (p. 60) that, '... when life or personhood begin ... are complex amalgams of factual and moral judgements. Instead of trying to answer these questions directly we have therefore gone straight to the question of how it is right to treat the human embryo.' The authors of the Warnock Report, like many others, prefer to duck the question by pretending that it is an unfathomable, philosophical subject. Yet amazingly, having not answered this big question and decided just when human life begins, and thus, the status of the human embryo, the Warnock Report pragmatically moves on to consider how the human embryo should be used and treated. This is bioethics at its worst and, of course, it results in evasion, deception, and macabre medicine and scary science. Yet this type of sloppy thinking is exactly how we got easy abortion, widespread human embryo abuse, and in general, the culture of death.

Thankfully, the Scriptures are clearer than much of our society's muddled thinking. But to begin with, two words of caution. First, the Bible is not a textbook of embryology, or gynaecology. That is not its purpose. Yet having said that, let us assert that the Bible does contain all that is necessary to guide us in all matters of truth, faith, and practice, and hence, in these bioethical issues too. In other words, the Bible is not exhaustive, but it is sufficient—it does not tell us everything, but it does tell us enough. Second, what follows is not an attempt at crude, or simplistic, 'proof-texting'. The Bible has a unity and its true meaning and teaching on any particular subject is determined, not on the weakness of an isolated verse or two, taken out of context, but on the strength of comparing and contrasting all of its contents, themes, and concepts. This is how Christian doctrines are properly constructed. When this exegetical pattern is followed, the effect of citing 'verse after verse' and 'text upon text' is that of generating an irresistible weight, or momentum, from the Scriptures. This exercise, when applied to the current question, will constrain us to conclude that the Scriptures teach that human life does indeed begin at no other time than at conception.

Less than ten passages of Scripture will be examined here, so, dear reader, you are being short-changed! But as you continue to read the Bible you will see for yourself, again and again, the same insistent theme— human life begins at conception.

For a start, God's benediction on our first parents, recorded in Genesis 1:28, 'Be fruitful and increase in number ...', was not rescinded by the Fall. Instead, we see it being continually fulfilled throughout the Scriptures. From Eve onwards (Genesis 4:1), conception is regarded as evidence of

God's continuing goodness to those who deserve no such thing. And the resulting children are seen as signs of God's grace and favour: '... children are a reward from him, like arrows...' and 'Blessed is the man whose quiver is full of them' (Psalm 127:3-5). But there is much, much more to consider.

Genesis 25:21-26 recounts the early life of Esau and Jacob. They were not just two vague non-entities, or collections of undifferentiated cells in the womb of Rebekah, but rather, they were already real, pre-born babies with real identities. In addition, we are introduced here to an awesome concept, the foreknowledge of God. In the foreknowledge of God, Esau and Jacob, these twin-brothers, were not even just two babies, but rather two nations, two peoples (Genesis 25:23)—here is redemptive history in the making, not on the battlefield, or at the temple, but in a womb! In this present section, we are contending that human life begins at conception, but in reality, from God's perspective, he has known all of us long, long before that. Such mysteries of foreknowledge and omniscience are beyond our full comprehension, but we bow to him and his Word.

This motif of the foreknowledge of God is repeated in Jeremiah 1:5. Here, God tells Jeremiah that, 'Before I formed you in the womb I knew you, before you were born I set you apart; I appointed you as a prophet to the nations.' Yes, God ordered Jeremiah's postnatal life (and ours too, which we are now living). Yes, but God also knew Jeremiah in his prenatal, pre-born life (and us in ours, too). Yes, Jeremiah had a real identity, at conception, (and so did we). Jeremiah was therefore known by God as man, foetus, embryo, and zygote, and even, in the foreknowledge of God, before that, before Jeremiah ever became a physical entity. The fact is, we all have a 'pre-history', but conception is when our earthly life started.

In Judges 13:1-7 an angel of God tells Samson's mother, 'You will conceive and give birth to a son.' She was then told, 'Now then, drink no wine or other fermented drink and do not eat anything unclean ...' Why these restrictions? Because her child-to-be, Samson, was to be a Nazirite and therefore such drink and food were never to enter his body, not even from across his mother's placenta. Why then, if the embryonic, or the foetal, or the pre-born Samson was not Samson proper, was his mother hedged about with such conditions during her pregnancy, and just to make sure, even before she conceived him? There is only one answer: because what was going to be in Manoah's wife's womb was going to be the actual Samson, tiny but undisguised—it was Samson from conception, Samson from day one.

Psalm 139:13-16 is a paean of praise from King David, as well as a ringing acknowledgement of God's creative involvement with all those made in his image, from day one and throughout 'all the days ordained for me'. David too, like us, was known by God from his earliest times. He reinforces this truth in Psalm 51:5, 'Surely I have been a sinner from birth, sinful from the time my mother conceived me.' Here we have the two-fold condition of man—sinner by practice *and* sinner by nature. When David was born, he committed sins—he became a sinner by practice. But before that, as soon as he was conceived, he became a sinner by nature. We too cannot help it—we commit sins, because we are sinners. When did we become sinners? As soon as we entered the human race. When did we enter the human race? As soon as we were conceived. *Quod erat demonstrandum*!

In Matthew 1:20 Joseph is told that, '... what is conceived in her [Mary] is from the Holy Spirit.' Here is the incarnation of the second person of the Trinity. The Lord Jesus Christ did not suddenly come down from heaven to appear in that feeding trough at Bethlehem. The incarnation was nine months earlier. Charles Wesley was not really correct when he wrote in his Christmas hymn, 'Our God contracted to a span, Incomprehensibly made man.' The Christ was once, like us, much smaller than a span, in fact he was as small, or even smaller than the fullstop at the end of this sentence. Now that is amazing! He came to share our humanity. He came as 'very God', but also as 'very Man'. He came as a real human being, like us in every way, except that he was without sin. As the writer to the Hebrews puts it, '... he had to be made like his brothers in every way ...' (Hebrews 2:17). Now then, since his earthly life began when he was conceived in Mary's womb, it is not a great leap of either reason or faith to conclude that you and I also began then, at our conception.

A few days after Joseph's remarkable visitation had occurred, Doctor Luke records yet another astonishing incident (Luke 1:39-45). Here Elizabeth, now six months pregnant with John the Baptist, is visited by the pregnant Mary, carrying the Christ-child, as a two-week-old embryo.

What an occasion it is when two happily pregnant women meet! But there is more here, because the unborn John the Baptist, previously promised (Luke 1:15) to be full of the Holy Spirit, undoubtedly hears the blessed Mary's greeting, but above and beyond that he recognizes that he is in the presence of the Son of God. And his response is what? To leap for joy! So, here are two unborn boys, who both demonstrate the deepest spiritual dimensions of what it means to be fully human and to bear the *imago Dei*. It is beyond cavil that the lives of John the Baptist and Jesus Christ had not only already begun, but were, in fact, in full developmental swing. Conception is but the start. Incidentally, although the Bible often calls attention to the event of a birth, as indeed we do with cards, parties, and repeated anniversaries, it draws no particular distinction between the unborn child and the born child. This continuity of prenatal and postnatal life is confirmed by the use of the same Greek word, *brephos*, for both, as, for example, in Luke 1:44 and Luke 2:12.

Finally, as any schoolboy who, as part of his religious education had to read the Authorized Version of the Bible will tell you, 'The Bible is full of begetting.' This somewhat archaic word describes the key role of the father in procreation—it is by 'fathering' that he passes on his genetic material to the next generation, how he achieves posterity, how he puts another branch into his genealogical tree. In one sense, he does nothing else during the next nine months, because the mother is the one involved in implantation, nutrition, gestation, labour, and birth. This emphasis on begetting (as found, for example, in Genesis 5 and Matthew 1) is synonymous with conception. It is when a man becomes a father, and a woman becomes a mother. The Bible declares and records it as a most notable event—two lives are changed, and another one is begun.

Scientifically, what happened at your conception, or what is sometimes equally referred to as fertilization? It was the union of just one sperm cell from your father and one egg cell from your mother. Each of these gametes contained twenty-three chromosomes and when they combined something wonderful happened. They were no longer just a sperm and an ovum, now they were a new cell, called, perhaps rather unattractively, a zygote. And that zygote contained all that was necessary for the unique individual that is you. Genetically, you were complete then. The only additional requirement you needed then, and indeed have done ever since then, has been nutrition. So, conception was the point that biblically, scientifically, and philosophically you started. It was the beginning of 'I'.

Since your conception, the only changes that have occurred have been in terms of development. The pattern has been this: zygote → morula → blastocyst → embryo → foetus → unborn child → newborn baby → infant → toddler → child → teenager → adult. This is the continuum of human life. Thus, human life begins not at birth, or at twenty-four weeks, or at eighteen weeks, or when brainwaves or blood are first detectable, or at implantation. The irrefutable fact is that we all began at conception as one cell, as a zygote, and that we spent the first nine months or so of our lives inside our mothers.

There is no disagreement here between the truth of the Bible and the truth of science—the one simply reinforces the other. The evidence is surely overwhelming.

2.3 Innocent human life is not to be taken

The Cain and Abel narrative (Genesis 4:8-12) demonstrates that human life is precious and sacred. The killing of animals was acceptable, but the killing of one made in God's image, namely, Abel, brought down divine anger: 'Your brother's blood cries out to me from the ground.' This first taking of a human life was an offence to a holy God.

The Sixth Commandment (Exodus 20 13; Deuteronomy 5:17) can be applied here too: 'You shall not murder.' That is, the deliberate taking of the life of another human being is wrong. Such an action violates God's law. Even the accidental killing of another human being was followed by a penalty (Numbers 35:6). The killer had to flee to a city of refuge. And if a house was to be built, the owner had to surround the flat roof with a parapet (Deuteronomy 22:8). Why? So that fellow human beings did not fall off and injure, or even kill, themselves. These were not punitive regulations, but rather expressions of God's caring concerns for those made in his image. He does not want any of us to come to harm.

The same Fatherly concern is expressed in Exodus 21:22-23. Some have made a meal of misinterpreting this passage claiming that it proves that the unborn child is less valuable than the mother, and therefore can be aborted. It does no such thing. The verses teach that if a man accidentally, that is, with no premeditated intent, struck a pregnant woman and this induced a premature, but safe birth of her child, there was to be a fine imposed. If she, or the child, died as a result of the incident, then it was 'life for life'. In other words, both mother *and* unborn child were precious and to be protected under the law. By contrast, consider how God must view the destruction of the unborn in that deliberate and pre-arranged manner that today is called abortion.

So, the Scriptures forbid the taking of innocent human life, whether it is pre-born or born, young or old. And in this context 'innocent' does not mean 'without sin', but rather it means 'without harm', that is, the embryo, foetus, child, or adult has committed no crime. So here is the Bible's clear prohibition on activities such as destructive human embryo experimentation, abortion, infanticide, and euthanasia.

Even the non-Christian arguments against these practices can be compelling. For many, it is a question of human rights—everyone has the right to life, it is the most basic of all rights. For others, it is a case of protecting the weak—defending and speaking for those who are unable to do so themselves. And for others, it is a matter of good medicine—it is simply rotten medical practice to kill your patient.

But for the Christian, with the Scriptures in his hand and the love of Christ in his heart, it is these biblical arguments that become irresistible and irrefutable.

2.4 All human life needs special care

We hear so much about abortion for the physically and the mentally disabled, or euthanasia for the senile and the elderly. And some Christians, though appalled by, for example, easy abortion, are confused and sometimes reticent to condemn these practices because of these so-called 'difficult' or 'hard' cases. So how can our thinking be biblically informed here?

To begin with, we need to remember that the unborn, the newborn with special needs, the Down's syndrome teenager, and the senile man are all human. They were made in the image and likeness of God, and they still bear the image and likeness of God.

The conversation between Moses and God recorded in Exodus 4:10-12 was a rebuke to Moses. God said, 'Who gave man his mouth? Who makes him deaf or dumb? Who gives him sight or makes him blind? Is it not I, the Lord?' Here is a mystery of providence. God sovereignly makes some of us particularly disabled. I do not fully understand why, and nor do you. Nevertheless, we are given a little insight in John 9:1-3, where a man, from his birth, was blind '... so that the work of God might be displayed in his life.' We should also note from verse 3 that such handicap is not the direct result of sin on the part of the sufferer, or of the parents—these words of the Lord Jesus Christ should dispel those wicked old wives' tales that have historically surrounded the issue of disability. Our understanding in this area is perhaps unclear, yet we must again bow before the teaching of Scripture and learn from its Author.

However, what is clear is that God does have a special concern for the welfare of the disabled. Leviticus 19:14 plainly warns, 'Do not curse the deaf or put a stumbling-block in front of the blind, but fear your God. I am the Lord.' And we know that the gentle Messiah would never break a bruised reed, nor would he ever snuff out a smouldering wick (Isaiah 42:3; Matthew 12:20). And we understand that it is in the weaknesses of humans that the power of God is displayed and made perfect (1 Corinthians 1:26-31; 2 Corinthians 12:9).

Yet, over and above even these comforts, there is still the great Christian hope—these handicaps, these disabilities, are but temporary. Isaiah 35:5-6 tells us that they will disappear in that Great Day: 'Then will the eyes of the blind be opened and the ears of the deaf unstopped. Then will the lame leap like a deer, and the tongue of the dumb shout for joy.'

Much of our ambivalence about disability, and those so affected, is rooted in this world's thinking. We have adopted the mindset of our age far too readily and we have become too cosy living within this culture of death. How many of us draw back when we are about to be hugged enthusiastically by the Down's syndrome boy? How many of us prefer to bypass the woman with senile dementia? We may put it down to British reserve, but for most of us, it is a shameful reminder that we too are part of our society's commitment to getting rid of such people. Why, our hospitals already have the most sophisticated screening programmes of prenatal diagnosis using, either amniocentesis, or chorion villus sampling (and in the near future, also preimplantation genetic diagnosis). When these techniques detect some genetic abnormality that may lead to handicap, no matter the degree of its severity, they are typically followed by abortion. And at the other end of the age spectrum, we are getting closer and closer to legalizing euthanasia, at least of the voluntary variety.

We have been too easily duped into thinking that this world is only for the 'big, the bright, and the beautiful'. This is one of the most dreadful and divisive aspects of our society—we think of ourselves as normal people, and we place ourselves in a group over here, and then there are the so-called handicapped, the disabled, as a sub-standard lot, in a group over there. And Christians are caught up in this new form of apartheid too. Those with special needs, need special care. We have forgotten about equality for all those made in the image of God. Shame on us!

Furthermore, ask this question: Who of us is *not* disabled? The truth is that we are all physically and mentally handicapped. None of us has unlimited physical strength or endurance, and as we become elderly we all become weaker and less agile—we really are all physically handicapped. Similarly, none of us has boundless mental abilities. Can you remember the date of your father's birthday, or, on a Monday morning, the preacher's three sermon points from the day before? Exactly! Nowadays most of us forget more than we learn—we really are all mentally handicapped. And even if you will not be convinced that you are mentally and physically disabled, then the Bible declares that you are handicapped, and hugely so, by sin—even the best of us has missed the mark, by a long, long way (Romans 3:23).

Finally, the real antidote to this sub-Christian thinking about disability is found in Isaiah 52:14. Here we have a prophetic glimpse of the suffering of the weak and disfigured Saviour. 'Just as there were many who were appalled at him—his appearance was so disfigured beyond that of any man and his form marred beyond human likeness.' Here he is, the Saviour of the world, the One whom probably most readers profess to love, follow, and serve. Here he is, hanging on the cross suffering for our sins in order that we might be brought back to God. So here is the pointed question: If you were there at Calvary, would you have drawn back from this physically-disabled man, this handicapped Saviour?

These are the four great themes from the Scriptures, the legs that together support this solid platform that will enable us to begin to think and to speak and to act, in short, to respond in a thoroughly biblical manner. So, now, what are these issues from the culture of death that need responding to?

Some of the primary issues

T hankfully, very few Christians need to become tip-top experts in bioethical issues. But that does not excuse any of us from attaining a decent understanding of the culture of death. If you want a realistic, minimum aim, then you should be able to talk sensibly about these issues over a cup of coffee (or tea) with a workmate, or your neighbour, or your cousin.

These issues are emotive. At times they generate more heat than light. I know—I was there when the pro-abortionists tried to wrench the doors off the Birmingham Town Hall during a packed pro-life rally. I have been harassed by screaming pro-choice feminists at university debating societies, and I have received hate mail from pro-death campaigners.

However, what we must recognize is that if we are to speak winsomely and with some authority we must get prepared. We need to learn to communicate coolly. We need to know some facts and figures. We also need to be able to refute some popular arguments. Therefore the following pages supply some background information to seven, fairly diverse, but current, bioethical issues. This information is general in its nature; it is not derived just from the Scriptures, because we must also strive to communicate with those outside the Christian community. This information is also purposely limited, to something like 1,500 words per topic, because it is intended as a launch pad to help get you started. Once started, you will begin to grow in knowledge and, hopefully, wisdom. Believe me, your second conversation, talk, or debate on any of these topics will be much better than your first!

3.1 Abortion

Schaeffer and Koop (1980) wrote (p. 19) in their magnificent book, *Whatever Happened to the Human Race?*, 'Of all the subjects relating to the erosion of the sanctity of human life, abortion is the keystone. It is the first and crucial issue that has been overwhelming in changing attitudes toward the value of life in general.' These authors were, and still are, spot on. Unless, and until, you have worked out your stance on abortion, you will settle little else in the realm of bioethical issues.

We can start by grasping two irrefutable facts. First, how many are aborted? Since the 1967 Abortion Act some 5 million unborn children have been aborted in the UK. The total number of abortions performed in England and Wales during 1999 was 183,250 (Office for National Statistics, 2000). This means that about 3,500 abortions occur every week, or almost 600 every working day, that is, every Monday, and every Tuesday, and every Wednesday, … Can you believe that? Sometimes I have to do the arithmetic again, just to check that huge daily figure—it is equivalent to about twenty classrooms, or about twelve coachloads of children each day. And remember, we are not talking about faraway places, like New York, Moscow, or Shanghai. This is happening where we live, and work, and go to church. Even so, abortion is not just limited to our neighbourhood; it is a global problem. For example, about 1.5 million abortions occur in the US each year and 0.5 million in Japan.

The second irrefutable fact relates to what is aborted. The 'favourite' time for abortion is nine to twelve weeks of gestation; half of the UK abortions occur at this developmental stage. Such an unborn child would fit snugly into the palm of your hand, she has eyes and fingernails, she moves, she swallows, she digests, she sucks her thumb. Blood has been coursing through her body for up to nine weeks, brainwaves have been detectable for as long as six weeks. We have been told that this is merely a vague collection of cells, or a little piece of poorly-defined tissue. What tosh! We have been duped. All abortions in England and Wales are now lawful up to twenty-four weeks. Yet premature babies of this age commonly survive. What a topsy-turvy world of medical ethics we live in—doctors can be fighting to preserve the life of a premature child in the intensive care unit, while down the corridor, in the same hospital, they can be destroying a child of a similar age. And if handicap is suspected, not necessarily proved, then abortion is lawful up to birth, yes, up to forty weeks. We, in the UK, have probably the most savage abortion law in the whole world.

So every abortion ends the life of a real, living, human being. We live in a society that puts to death its young, and even claims that there is virtue in doing so—we are told that abortion is done for the good of the mother, or for the good of the child, or for both. Furthermore, our taxes and our votes support abortion. And if we say and do nothing, then our hearts and minds condone such a shabby public policy.

Abortion has had a profound and deleterious effect upon our society. It has confounded the unique role of women in the bearing and caring of children—we have asked women to be gentle and compassionate, yet abortion changes these expectations. Their peers, doctors, husbands, and boyfriends tell women that abortion is 'for them', but in reality abortion is 'against them'. It has physically and psychologically damaged many, many women—post-abortion syndrome is now recognized as a major medical condition. No woman gets away from abortion scot-free.

Abortion has distorted the family, that centre of safety, nurture, and love in our society, yet it is right there that abortion is often decided upon. Family members are often the victims of the abortion conspiracy, namely, that 'abortion is simple'. Yet for many it brings guilt, remorse and long-term grief. Abortion can create an immediate void in the parents' lives. There is not only foetal loss, there is a real loss for real parents—a man and a woman have irrevocably become a father and a mother—and for some, even though their child is dead, abortion can become a major death experience.

Abortion has abrogated the traditional role of men as protectors of women and children. It has subverted that most deep and complex of relationships, namely, that between a child and a parent—abortion abruptly ends this. It has caused uncertainty in the minds of born children—was I ever meant to be? It has frustrated the hopes and roles of grandparents. It has helped undermine marriage because it has been used to 'correct' the 'errors' of adultery and fornication.

Abortion never occurs in a relationship vacuum—abortion is the result of failed relationships. It has produced a new selfishness because abortion 'for the sake of the child' is really for the sake of the mother and father. So, we may well ask, when did abortion ever produce, or strengthen family relationships? Abortion does not solve any problems, it usually exchanges one set for another.

The advent of easy access to abortion has, in part, been the cause of a huge decline in the number of adoptions; in 1968 there were 27,000 adoptions in the UK, in 1992 there were only 8,000. Adoption, with its

Biblical precedents (such as, 2 Samuel 9 and even Galatians 4:4-7; Ephesians 1:5), used to be the route by which many infertile couples raised a family. Now it has become a virtual cul-de-sac.

Abortion has wrecked the historic foundations of medical ethics and practice, namely, the Christian doctrines and the Hippocratic oath. To kill those made in the image of God is an affront to the Creator and it makes a nonsense of the Bible's golden rule. How can the Hippocratic dictum, 'Do no patient any harm', be reconciled with the practice of abortion? And because abortion is now such a routine part of obstetrics and gynaecology training and practice, many morally-sensitive doctors and nurses, among the best we have, are excluded from making careers in these areas.

But its effects have been even wider—we have all been affected. For example, abortion has hardened our attitude and blunted our compassion towards the weak. The 'search-and-destroy' practice that is directed against the unborn disabled has fostered an ambivalence in our society towards the born disabled. It has eased the way for the next logical development, infanticide. Furthermore, how can our attitude and response to Third World devastation, deprivation, and famine ever be adequate when we have such a cheap view of human life at home?

When any society regards, and therefore begins to treat, human life as a cheap and disposable commodity, history teaches us that the outcome is always bad. Our society has persisted in putting to death its unborn offspring, who are among the most precious of our legacies, and the full cost of such a public policy has yet to be reckoned, let alone paid.

3.2 In vitro fertilization (IVF)

IVF is one of the group of assisted reproductive techniques (ARTs), which includes other procedures like, artificial insemination and surrogacy. IVF came to the attention of the public with the birth of Louise Brown, the world's first 'test-tube' baby, on 25 July 1978 in Oldham, Lancashire.

Much of the impetus behind the development of ARTs has been for the treatment of infertility. Infertility is not uncommon and generally estimated to affect 1 in 6 couples. It is usually associated with either damaged, or blocked, Fallopian tubes in women, or a low sperm count in men. But there are many, many other minor causes, such as alcohol abuse, stress, and sexually-transmitted diseases, like the surprisingly, even fright-eningly, widespread *Chlamydia trachomatis*. While there is no doubt that infertility can cause deep psychological distress in some people (as recorded in several biblical narratives, including those of Sarai in Genesis 16, and Rachel in Genesis 30), few would maintain that every couple has the right to children. Such a concept is certainly foreign to the biblical worldview, which maintains that God is sovereign in both infertility (1 Samuel 1:5) and fertility (Luke 1:36-37).

In the early 1980s it became clear that the fast-moving technology of the ARTs was outstripping our bioethical, legal, and social thinking. Technology was remaking parenthood. It used to be common knowledge that a baby had just one mother and one father. This is no longer so. Now a baby can have as many as five parents—for example, in a surrogacy arrangement there might be commissioning, genetic, and biological mothers, plus commissioning and genetic fathers. The whole ART's enterprise was becoming uncontrollably complex, and in some cases, defi-nitely bizarre. To counter this the then Conservative government set up, in July 1982, a Committee of Inquiry into Human Fertilisation and Embryology, chaired by Dame (now Baroness) Mary Warnock. The Committee's terms of reference were: 'To consider recent and potential developments in medicine and science related to human fertilisation and embryology; to consider what policies and safeguards should be applied, including consideration of the social, ethical and legal implications of these developments; and to make recommendations.' The landmark Warnock Report was published, two years later, in July 1984.

The Warnock Report addressed the UK situation, but it was a global forerunner; the world was looking on for clear bioethical statements and practical guidance. However, the Report turned out to be a dog's breakfast. Its thinking was, in too many places, muddled and shallow and it often avoided the major issues, or fudged them. The Warnock Report has thus become one of the most influential examples of unprincipled, utilitarian thinking of the last century, yet its bioethical reach has extended firmly into this century too.

Basically, the Report recommended that IVF should be generally available, regardless of whose gametes were involved, with no restriction on the supply, use, sale, or purchase of eggs, semen, or embryos and no restriction on egg donation, sperm-freezing, and the production of multiple 'spare' embryos. All this was to be regulated by a statutory licensing body, now called the Human Fertilisation and Embryology Authority (HFEA). The HFEA has been little more than a group of 'poachers turned gamekeepers' because its members have always been IVF practitioners and human embryo experimenters, or at least, supporters of such activities. There has not been a single pro-life voice on any of its committees—I applied to join during the initial trawl for members, but I never even received a reply! Also the Report recommended that human embryos produced in vitro must not be kept alive for more than fourteen days, and whereas they could be specifically created for research, such embryos must not be transferred back to a woman. Most of these recommendations were incorporated into the Human Fertilisation and Embryology Act 1990.

Some consider that the whole of IVF is artificial and that this technological 'making' of children is morally unacceptable. Children as laboratory products is an uneasy concept. It must certainly be conceded that it is very different from normative parenthood, where a child is the result of life expressed in the procreative act of married union and therefore has much to do with deep human integrity and profound human relationships. This view has strong ethical, theological, and sociological reasoning, but the Warnock Report virtually ignored it.

Other areas of continuing controversy concern some of the specific practices associated with IVF. There are many variations on the IVF theme. For example, there is GIFT (gamete intra-fallopian transfer), whereby ovum and sperm are mixed and replaced into the Fallopian tubes with the idea that fertilization will occur in its 'natural' environment. There is also ICSI (intracytoplasmic sperm injection), which is used in certain cases of male infertility when sperm are unable to penetrate the zona pellucida, or outer layer of the ovum—ICSI overcomes this inability by injecting one sperm directly into the cytoplasm of the ovum.

But to return to straightforward IVF. A typical protocol involves the collection of an ovum, which is checked and if it looks satisfactory, then sperm is mixed with it in a glass (Latin, *vitrum*, hence, *in vitro* fertilization) dish and the contents are incubated at 37°C for about three days. If fertilization, which is not inevitable, occurs the 3-day-old embryo is again examined before being placed (note, not *replaced* or *implanted*, as many journalists and broadcasters still erroneously insist) in the woman's womb. Here, implantation, which again is not inevitable, may occur. Perhaps the majority would find this type of IVF acceptable for the relief of infertility of a married couple where, say, the woman had blocked Fallopian tubes. But this 'one for one' replacement routinely occurs in no IVF clinics in the UK. The success rates of IVF procedures are terribly poor—Louise Brown was attempt number 104. Even now, after more than twenty years of IVF, the likelihood of a 'take home' baby, or as the HFEA defines it, a 'live birth event', averages only 18 per cent. Put the other way, IVF generally has an 80+ per cent failure rate.

To increase the likelihood of success, IVF clinics super-ovulate women, that is, they treat women with a regime of fertility drugs so that she produces as many as ten or even twenty ova, instead of the normal one each month. The 'best' of these ova are then mixed with sperm so that many human embryos are produced. Typically, the 'best' three embryos (the maximum number currently allowed in the UK) are transferred to the woman's womb. This can lead to the problem of multiple pregnancies. Almost half (forty-seven per cent) of all IVF babies come from multiple pregnancies, which are associated with maternal health problems, low birth weights, high rates of stillbirth, neonatal deaths, and long-term disabilities. These risks of multiple pregnancies have been minimized by the horrors of 'selective reduction', whereby a number of the siblings are killed by piercing their hearts, in utero.

Super-ovulation treatment can cause ovarian hyperstimulation syndrome (OHSS) in a few women. More commonly, it produces poor quality eggs that often do not fertilize, and also a uterine environment that is unfavourable for embryo implantation. This latter problem can be circumvented by freezing the embryos and transferring them to a menstrual cycle or two later, when the woman's hormonal balance is more favourable. Herein is the problem of scrutiny, assessment, selection, and transfer of only the 'best' embryos. This is nothing other than QC (quality control) for human beings. Embryos are therefore inevitably discarded from IVF procedures because there are too many, or because, for some other reason, they are deemed unsuitable. After all, what doctor would dare transfer a less than seemingly 'perfect' human embryo into a woman's womb?

And so there is the problem of these surplus, or 'spare' embryos. They have three fates: they may be frozen, or experimented upon, or thrown away. Ask one of those fundamental questions: Is this any way to treat live, human beings? At least three points need to be considered. First, is this 'spare' embryo, human? There is really no doubt here. Can the fruit of human gametes be anything other than human? The embryo certainly cannot be that of a dog, or a donkey. Second, is this human embryo, alive? The Warnock Report (p. 58) states: 'At fertilisation the egg and sperm unite to become a single cell.' It then explains how this zygote multiplies and diversifies rapidly and spontaneously. If the embryo were not alive, this would be inexplicable—this very growth is diagnostic of the fact that the embryo is alive. Third, is this alive, human embryo, 'one of us'? As we have already noted, the Warnock Report (p. 60) prevaricates at this crucial question: '... when life or personhood begin ... are complex amalgams of factual and moral judgements.' Ah, how the simple can become so complex! Warnock ducked this issue. But we already know the answer, do we not?

IVF brings with it other bioethical dilemmas too. What about grandmothers giving birth to their grandchildren? What about post-menopausal women having babies? What about posthumous fatherhood? Such strange, unnatural events have already occurred around the world because of IVF.

But the far more commonplace nightmare is the fact that IVF clinics are destroying thousands and thousands of human embryos each year. By early 1998 the number of human embryos created in the IVF units of UK hospitals and clinics was a staggering 763,499. Yet only 36,317 of these embryos had resulted in a born baby. That is a mere 4.75 per cent. At least 90 per cent of the 763,499 were already dead. They had been thrown away because they were 'sub-standard', or 'surplus to requirements'. Others were wasted because they were experimented on up to the fourteen-day legal limit, and others would have been the result of failed IVF treatments. The remainder were frozen in liquid nitrogen (an indignity, which can never be a proper way to treat live, human beings) and thousands would have been killed by either this process, or the subsequent thawing process. Others would have been destroyed because they had reached the end of their five- or ten-year statutory storage period. Many of those destroyed will have been 'orphaned'. Why? Because the clinics have lost contact with the parents, labels have dropped off the embryo storage vessels, records have been misplaced, or lost, or not updated so that some of the embryos' parents, who have divorced, died, or simply moved house, cannot now be traced. It has all become a double disaster, a bioethical and an administrative calamity.

Lastly, there is the problem of the costs of IVF. The costs are both financial (about £2,000 to £3,000 per treatment cycle) and psychological (typically characterized by stress, and sometimes by relationship failure between the couple, and with gamete-donating third parties). You might think all this would be enough to make anyone fear and flee from getting involved with IVF. But you would be wrong. According to the HFEA Annual Report (2000), as many as 27,151 women received IVF treatment in the seventy-five clinics throughout the UK during the year ending November 1999. A total of 35,363 treatment cycles were started, of which 30,520 reached the stage of embryo transfer. These in turn produced 7,762 clinical pregnancies (defined as ultrasound evidence of a foetal heart), which resulted in 6,450 'live birth events'.

The HFEA then assesses IVF performance as 'live birth events' per hundred treatment cycles started, so the UK clinics' average 'success rate' in 1999 was just 18.2 per cent. But even this overestimates the efficacy of IVF. The picture is muddied because not all treatment cycles produce embryos, or even ova. In addition, one 'live birth event' can count for the delivery of a singleton, twins, or triplets. A better performance indicator would be the number of children born per hundred embryos transferred. When this is calculated, from the data in Table 4.8 of the HFEA Annual Report (2000), the figure is a measly 11.7 per cent. This means that almost nine out of every ten human embryos created for IVF, die by IVF. The true picture is numerically, and certainly bioethically, even worse because, as already noted, only a small proportion of all the embryos created are actually transferred. It is hard to square all this wastage with the Warnock

Report's recommendation (p. 63), '... that the embryo of the human species should be afforded some protection in law.'

So what has IVF achieved? Of course, some lovely bouncing babies. But more importantly it has reintroduced the era of 'the end justifies the means', especially with human embryos. It has produced a view of human life that is pretty cold, if not chilling, where human ova, sperm, embryos are little more than laboratory materials. Where human sexuality is simply a biological phenomenon, controlled by technicians. It is a prescription for a clinical, dehumanized world where there is not much awe, little reverence, and virtually no dignity. In short, IVF has further encouraged the trivialization of human life and hastened the spread of the culture of death.

3.3 Human embryo experimentation

The culture of death is also part of human embryo experimentation because this is almost always destructive—it is seldom performed for the good of the patient. Furthermore, it is inextricably linked to in vitro fertilization (IVF); the latter supplies its 'spare', or surplus embryos as the biological material for the experimentation.

The use of human embryos in experimental research was approved by the controversial Warnock Report (1984), though seven of its sixteen Committee members were against it in some form or other and the Report includes their two Expressions of Dissent (pp. 90-94). Nevertheless, the Report produced two arguments in favour of the practice. The first argument (p. 62) concerns the status of the embryo, 'A human embryo cannot be thought of as a person, or even a potential person. It is simply a collection of cells which, unless it implants in a human uterine environment, has no potential for development.' And it continues (p. 62), 'There is no reason therefore to accord these cells any protected status.' Therefore, Warnock recommends (p. 64) '... that research on human in vitro embryos ... should be permitted ...' The first objection to these statements is that 'potential' is a dangerous word. It can lead to serious understatement. A human embryo is not merely a 'potential' human, it is already a real, actual one. We were all once embryos. Second, an adult can be described as, 'simply a collection of cells'. This may be just about the ultimate in reductionism, but it does contain a certain truth. Third, an embryo does have *potential* for development, but not the *opportunity* if it is not inserted into a woman's womb—the Report muddled these two words.

The second of Warnock's arguments in favour of embryo experimentation is connected with respect and protection. The Report (p. 62) states, 'We found that the more generally held position, however, is that though the human embryo is entitled to some added measure of respect beyond that accorded to other animal subjects, that respect cannot be absolute ...' Hence, human embryos can be used as laboratory material. Instead of offering a well-thought out, rigorously-argued case, the Warnock Report plumps for 'the more generally held position'. But since when has the 'generally held position' been the measure of what is right and proper? You and I know!

So, according to the Warnock Report, the human embryo is a 'sort of' human being, worthy of some respect and protection. This is all uneasy stuff. Back in the mid-1980s the bioethical world was watching and waiting for some definitive answers to these big questions, but instead of delivering the goods, the Warnock Report preferred to dodge, duck, and deflect. Sadly, since its publication, the Report has set the agenda and provided the quasi-arguments for much of the world's thinking and practice concerning human embryo experimentation.

The champions of human embryo research have always insisted that such experimentation is essential for three main reasons: to increase the success rate of IVF, to provide treatments for genetic diseases, and to improve contraceptive methods. After almost two decades, human embryo experimentation has actually achieved very little. In truth, it is not needed. There are other ways of, for example, treating many types of infertility without resorting to IVF and experimenting with human embryos. Similarly, the development of new treatments and cures for genetic disorders, such as by somatic gene therapy, do not require the use of embryos as experimental subjects. Research into methods of contraception (as opposed to abortifacient methods) is properly directed at either sperm or ova, not human embryos. Anyway, most so-called 'contraceptive failure' is associated with simple misuse by men and women. These alternatives to human embryo experimentation may be somewhat slower to develop, and they may be less glitzy and less newsworthy, but they are certainly less offensive to the morally-sensitive.

Finally, the recommendations of the Warnock Report concerning human embryo experimentation, and their incorporation into the Human Fertilisation and Embryology Act 1990, have resulted in three novel, but awful practices. First, we have publicly accepted, for the first time, that human beings can be the subject of research and experimentation that is not for their own benefit, and without their consent. This is a frightening departure from traditional medical ethics. Second, we have created a new crime, that of keeping a human being alive *after* fourteen days, the upper limit for embryo research proposed by the Warnock Report. For the first time it is a crime *not* to kill a fellow human being. Third, we have created a new race of human beings. They are created in laboratories, they never leave laboratories, and they are killed in laboratories. Is this not the last word in exploitation and manipulation of human life?

3.4 Human cloning

One of the current hottest topics in bioethics is an offshoot of embryo experimentation; it is cloning. The general public has a fascination with it, especially human cloning. On 25 February 1998, the *Daily Mirror* contained the headline, 'Plans to Clone Elvis Presley from His Toenail.' A group called ACE (Americans for Cloning Elvis) had gathered 3,000-plus signatures on a petition urging the use of Elvis' DNA, to be obtained from one of his toenails collected by a fan, to produce his double. In a poll the following year, Mother Teresa of Calcutta was voted as the most popular choice for cloning, closely followed by Michelle Pfeiffer!

However, the more serious aspects of cloning came to the world's attention on 5 July 1996, when, in a shed just outside Edinburgh, a mother gave birth to a 6.6 kg offspring. It was a snow-white Finn-Dorset lamb called 6LL3, or more popularly, Dolly.

Cloning is technically complex, but is bioethically simple. There are two techniques used for cloning. First, there is embryo splitting. This occurs naturally in the womb and produces monozygotic, or identical, twins. Embryo splitting can also be induced artificially in the laboratory.

Thus, individual cells could be removed from an early human embryo, say, a sixteen-cell morula. These cells could be cultured in the laboratory, biologically reprogrammed and stimulated to divide, and eventually they would result in identical embryos, or clones.

Second, there is cell nuclear replacement (CNR), also known as cell nuclear transfer. There is no natural equivalent to this. The nucleus, which contains the genetic material, is removed from a body cell, perhaps a skin or a liver cell, taken from the animal, or perhaps in the near future, the human patient, to be cloned. This nucleus is then transferred, as a replacement, into a donated ovum, from the same species, which is non-nucleated, that is, from which the nucleus has previously been excised. Again, culturing, reprogramming, and stimulation are required to produce an embryonic clone. And, because sperm is not needed in CNR, the technique could signal the end of men in human reproduction and the subsequent upbringing of children!

CNR is not new, it has been used for the last fifty years to, for example, clone frogs from tadpole cells. However, what was significant about Dolly was that she was the first mammal to be cloned by CNR using an *adult* cell from another animal, namely, an udder cell from a six-year-old sheep. Even so, the technique is far from efficient because 277 reconstructed sheep embryos were produced at the Roslin Institute by Professor Wilmut and his team, of which only 13 survived and of these, which were transferred to host wombs, only one, Dolly, went to term.

There are two purposes for cloning, and specifically human cloning. And it makes no difference whether the embryos are obtained from embryo splitting, or CNR, or even as 'spare' embryos from IVF treatments.

First, there is therapeutic cloning. The cells of fertilized ova, namely, zygotes, as well as those of early embryos, have a most amazing property—they are, in the word used in the Warnock Report (p. 58), 'totipotential'. That is, these cells, known as stem cells, have the ability to multiply and to develop into all the different types of cells required for the human body; perhaps they will become brain, skin, bone, spleen, or fingernails. As their development proceeds these 'totipotent' cells become 'pluripotent' and then 'multipotent' signifying their greater specialization and lessening ability to change into other cells, organs, and tissues. Nevertheless, all of these stem cells retain a prodigious capacity to divide and to be transformed.

Therapeutic cloning would artificially harness this natural property of stem cells. It would take cells, say skin cells, from a human patient, clone them by CNR to produce human embryos. The embryos' stem cells would be collected, though the process would destroy the embryos. These stem cells would then be used to produce other types of cell, perhaps nerve cells, or to regenerate spare tissues, perhaps cardiac muscles, or even bodily parts, perhaps a hip joint. The much-heralded motive behind this therapeutic cloning is that the cells produced could be used to replace a patient's diseased, or damaged cells and thus conquer diseases like Alzheimer's, Parkinson's, leukaemia, and diabetes. Therapeutic cloning means that the cells, the tissues, or the organs produced would be histocompatible, that is, there would be no problems of tissue rejection because they would be genetically identical to the patient's originals.

Second, there is reproductive cloning. Today this is widely used for farm animals such as, sheep, pigs, and calves. One fear is that it may be used tomorrow for humans. Human reproductive cloning is currently illegal in the UK, but the required embryos could still be legally prepared here and transported to a country where reproductive cloning is not illegal. Already people are interested in this form of cloning for several, typically selfish, reasons. Copying themselves, they say, would ensure their own 'immortality'. Families may wish to replace a dead loved one, or bereaved parents may wish to replace a 'lost' child. Infertile couples could use the technique to have children, who would be genetically linked to them, instead of using donated gametes. Lesbian couples could transfer genetic material from one woman to the other's ovum; the women would then both be biological mothers to the child.

Human cloning should make us nervous. Its ethics tend to be totally utilitarian and utterly self-serving. They are part of the scientific imperative: 'We have the technology, so why not use it?' But cloning could engender significant class, economic, and power differences within our society. It could create an underclass of people, who are unable to enhance or choose their offsprings' genes, and so they would become more and more genetically unattractive. These are the typical, unsavoury outcomes of any such selective breeding programmes, or what is plainly known as old-fashioned eugenics.

But our primary objection to both therapeutic and reproductive cloning must be that they result in the exploitation and the deliberate destruction of human embryos. It is only the purpose that distinguishes therapeutic from reproductive cloning—the former may continue for up to fourteen days on the researcher's laboratory bench, the latter up to nine months in the womb of a surrogate mother. It is always wrong to use any human life as a means to an end—it is utilitarianism. It is that culture of death again.

However, it seems that the objectives of therapeutic cloning need not be a 'no-go' area. Its benefits can be achieved without this wholesale destruction of human embryos. Recent research from the USA, Sweden, and elsewhere has shown that adult tissues (and even umbilical cords), retain some stem cells, and surprisingly, and contrary to accepted biological dogma, these can be reprogrammed to generate a broad range of different cells and tissues. In other words, stem cells from adults, rather than from human embryos, can be used to achieve the perceived benefits of therapeutic cloning. So, stem cell therapies that require the destruction of human embryos could already be redundant. A better way forward had been found.

In August 2000, the long-awaited Donaldson Committee Report recommended to Parliament that reproductive cloning should become illegal, but that research into therapeutic cloning be allowed. The latter was almost exclusively discussed in terms of stem cells derived from human embryos, obtained by either of the two cloning techniques, or from the 'spares' generated by IVF procedures. The possibility of using stem cells from adults was largely ignored. Why? Because scientists want to perfect the CNR technique so that they can use it in reproductive cloning? Because they are fascinated only by experimenting with human embryos? Because the scientific imperative makes them thirst for the big breakthrough with its attendant publicity, kudos, and power?

Such a blinkered approach to progress in science and medicine is reprehensible. But it is not only the Donaldson Committee that has virtually dismissed adult stem cell work. The world-famous National Institutes of

Health in the USA has too. It has argued that, 'Adult stem cells are often present in only minute quantities, are difficult to isolate and purify, and their numbers may decrease with age.' Yet on the very day the Donaldson Report was released (16 August 2000), *The Times* carried news from a group in New Jersey which had used stem cells, isolated from adult bone marrow, and transformed them into nerve cells. The group's spokesman, Dr Ira Black, said, 'These cells grow like wildfire in culture, so we have a virtually unlimited supply.' These two statements are quite incompatible. Stem cell science is moving so fast—there was just a three-month gap between these two statements—yet if it is going to be monopolized by those from the culture of death then it will never become a praiseworthy venture.

Now the British Parliament has gone one step further and implemented the recommendations of the Donaldson Committee. In December 2000, the House of Commons, followed in January 2001 by the House of Lords, approved an extension to the Human Fertilisation and Embryology Act 1990 to include the use of human embryos for research into therapeutic cloning. Britain thus became the first, and only, country in Europe to permit human cloning. This was despite an appeal against such a move from the European Parliament, and despite the fact that other countries have already banned this work. Parliamentary debate on the ominous link between therapeutic and reproductive cloning was again blurred, little was said about embryo destruction, and the entire discussion, on such a weighty bioethical issue, was unduly rushed.

Much of the pro-cloning lobby has tried to steal the high moral ground by entirely rejecting human cloning of the reproductive variety—'It's abhorrent', they say. Indeed, it has gone even further—it now rejects *all* human cloning because it has renamed therapeutic cloning as cell nuclear replacement (CNR). Thus, the dreaded 'C' word can be sidestepped and the general public can be insulated from the fact that CNR is used in all forms of cloning, reproductive and therapeutic. Furthermore, those opposed to obtaining stem cells from human embryos are now accused of depriving people with debilitating diseases of possible cures.

The fact is, we do not want, or even need, human cloning. Instead, we should welcome adult stem cell research; it is a new and revolutionary approach to medicine, yet it is also bioethically uncontroversial. We are not anti-science, or anti-research, or anti-progress. But we do insist that science and medicine are practised within a wholesome bioethical framework, firmly rooted within the culture of life.

3.5 Human genetic engineering

Genetic engineering rests on three great pieces of science. In about 1860, that Augustinian monk, Gregor Mendel reported something of the mechanisms of genetic inheritance after experimenting with his garden peas. In 1953, James Watson and Francis Crick described the three-dimensional structure of the double helix of deoxyribonucleic acid (DNA), the carrier of the genetic code. Then in 2000, a huge international team of scientists, working on the Human Genome Project, 'cracked' the human genetic code, that is, they sequenced the human genome. This has been declared as one of the greatest feats of modern science—we should not underestimate it.

Each somatic cell (as opposed to each gamete, or germ cell, which is either sperm, or ovum) of our bodies contains forty-six chromosomes (germ cells contain only twenty-three), and collectively these are known as the human genome. Together these chromosomes contain perhaps as many as 40,000 genes. So each gene is basically a short length of DNA within one of these forty-six chromosomes. The biological significance of a gene is that it specifies, or codes for, the synthesis of a particular protein. And the significance of a protein is two-fold. First, it can be a structural 'building block' of our bodies, as a major component of muscles, organs, blood, hair, and so on. Or second, it can be a metabolic 'controller' of our bodies, in the form of an enzyme, or a hormone. Therefore, to a large extent, our genes determine who we are, at least, in the physical sense—1.8 metres tall, brown eyes, mousy hair, size nine feet, well, that is partly who I am, as a result of my genes.

Every one of the estimated 10,000 billion somatic cells in a human body contains the human genome as about two metres of ultra-thin, super-coiled DNA. Therefore, every human adult contains about 20 billion kilometres of the stuff. Amazed? So am I. And this DNA contains our genetic message as a series of just four nucleotide bases, known in shorthand by the letters A, T, G, and C. These are arranged in pairs on the double helix of DNA as AT, TA, GC, or CG. There are about 3,300 million of these base pairs in the human genome and the Human Genome Project has determined the sequence of this enormous genetic alphabet—it is a technological marvel. When King David wrote in Psalm 139:14, '... I am fearfully and wonderfully made; your works are wonderful ...', he did not know the half of it!

Now that we understand so much about the mechanisms of inheritance and gene function we are just beginning to alter and control these genes with considerable precision. Much of the impetus for this human genetic engineering has come from the hope of curing genetic diseases. First, we need to understand the true meaning of terms like treatment, cure, and prevention. Most genetic diseases can be treated, a few can be cured, but prevention, at least within the culture of death, often means destroying the patient, such as the unborn child with Down's syndrome, who is detected by prenatal diagnosis, and then killed by abortion. This is nothing other than squalid, modern-day eugenics.

The eugenics movement was started in an organized way by Francis Galton, who, interestingly, was Charles Darwin's cousin. In 1883 he first used the word eugenics (from the Greek, *eu*, well and *genes*, born) to mean improvement of the human species by genetic means. This included the elimination of genetic diseases, plus the enhancement of desirable traits.

In 1908, Galton formed the Eugenics Society in London to investigate human heredity and to carry out social action programmes. Altruism may have motivated some of its members, but race, class, and privilege were the issues for other members, that is, superiority and inferiority, racial and ethnic prejudice were on their agenda. Eugenics has often been linked with nationalism. Certainly, Hitler and the Nazis carried eugenic thinking to its cruel extreme with sterilization programmes that championed Aryan elitism, followed by the Final Solution of the Holocaust.

For many years the early eugenicists propagated an astonishingly simple error. They thought that mental handicap could be eliminated if they segregated, or sterilized, affected people, that is, stopped them from reproducing. But such a practice is confuted by the Hardy-Weinberg principle (*Nature*, 23 March 1995, 374:302-304), which not only demonstrated the ineffectiveness of their eugenic schemes, but it also destroyed their daft ideals. Nevertheless, eugenicists still abound today, but their science is not as shoddy as that of their predecessors, and they are less naive, and more disguised. Certain eugenic motives are involved in some of the new reproductive technologies, as well as some of the commonly-accepted medical practices, such as antenatal, or prenatal, screening—a procedure that *Nature* (14 April 1994, 368:572) rightly called 'eugenics of a mild sort'.

So historically, human genetic engineering has a pretty shabby pedigree. Yet modern-day genetic engineering has enormous potential for good, that is, if only it could be practised within the culture of life. But it comes not without bioethical tensions, especially when practised within the culture of death. These tensions can be seen, for example, when genetic engineering techniques are used to screen people for genetic diseases. Screening can be a can of worms. One of the earliest screening programmes was for sickle cell anaemia in the US during the 1970s. It went disastrously wrong and resulted in discrimination and unfair employment dismissals because of inaccuracies in the analytical techniques used. There were too many false-positives and false-negatives, that is, people without sickle cell anaemia were told they had it, and those with it were told they were in the clear.

But genetic screening need not be all bad. For example, if screening could tell us what genetic diseases we were prone to, and likely to develop in later life, then we could adapt our lifestyle. 'Predisposition' is the buzzword. If we were predisposed to say, heart disease, then we could devise a personalized life-plan, 'do this, don't do that', and thus avoid some of its associated risks. On the other hand, screening can have a huge downside. Our employers will want us screened to ensure that we are not likely to leave them in the lurch by taking early retirement on medical health grounds, or even dying prematurely. Our insurance and mortgage companies will also want to know the diseases to which we are predisposed. The results of genetic screening may influence whom we marry. Having children may become more controlled if screening of both parents and their offspring, in the form of prenatal genetic diagnosis in conjunction with IVF, were to become more prevalent.

Today's standard screening methods, for say, cervical or breast cancer, rely on microscopic or x-ray examinations of cells and tissues rather than on genetic testing, but these current methods are complex, somewhat unreliable, and even of doubtful utility. Future, genetically-based, screening methods may be more akin to pregnancy testing—pop along to the chemist, buy a kit, and simply test your own blood, or urine, or saliva in the comfort of your own home. Not so long ago such relatively simple genetic testing was predicted to become the method of choice for the screening of diseases caused by a single faulty gene, such as in severe combined immunodeficiency (SCID), or in cystic fibrosis. But reality has proved to be more complex. Now even the single gene for cystic fibrosis, called CFTR, is known to have several hundred mutations and therefore can cause many forms of the disease, with quite different symptoms, and severities. Each mutation requires its own specific genetic test, so which mutation do you test for? But reality has proved to be even much more complex. Most genetic diseases, like the various types of breast and colon cancer, are not single, but multiple gene disorders, caused by the inter-action of several genes. Others, like Down's syndrome, are disorders relating to whole chromosomes. We know very, very little about such complexities. And, of course, even the best genetic testing will indicate little more than a 'predisposition' to a particular disease—it will not necessarily confirm that the carrier will ever develop the disorder. In fact, we are all carriers of many gene defects—for example, about one in twenty-five people are carriers of the cystic fibrosis gene—but most of us, including our children, will never express these particular diseases for various reasons, including our spouse's genetic make-up, as well as other factors like, lifestyle, environment, and diet.

In all, there are some 1,500 known gene defects—some are trivial, but some are not. About 7,000 babies a year are born with them in the UK, including 1,000 with Down's syndrome, 400 with cystic fibrosis, and 100 with Duchenne's muscular dystrophy. Antenatal screening, in the form of amniocentesis and chorion villus sampling, has been widely used for many years, but the incidence of babies born with these gene defects has remained largely unchanged. So will the advent of preimplantation genetic diagnosis (PGD), with its battery of modern techniques, namely, a combination of IVF, embryo biopsy, and chromosomal analysis, significantly reduce the numbers affected? Probably not, for three reasons.

First, there are about 630,000 children born in the UK each year. Would their parents be likely to relinquish sexual intercourse for the procedures of the IVF clinic? No. Second, would the already overburdened NHS cope with such mass screening? Probably not. Third, would the selection of couples at risk decrease the incidence of these genetic defects? Possibly not. For example, the risk of Down's syndrome increases with maternal age. So why not screen those at increased risk, say, the over thirty-five-year-old pregnant women? About 31,500 women in this age group give birth each year in the UK. Such a screening policy, linked to abortion, would prevent some Down's babies being born, but each year 700 such children are born to mothers *under* thirty-five years of age. Or consider Duchenne's muscular dystrophy. The gene for this is female-carried, but the clinical condition affects only male offspring. A carrier female has a one-in-two risk of producing an affected son and the same risk of producing a carrier daughter. Comprehensive screening of all the women relatives of already-affected boys would identify carriers and they could be offered IVF plus embryo biopsy and chromosomal analysis to identify the affected and carrier embryos—these would then be destroyed. But even this would not eradicate Duchenne's because about thirty per cent of cases occur by spontaneous mutation.

Similar bioethical problems exist with genetic screening for cystic fibrosis. Something like eighty-five per cent of cases are caused by one of four commonly-occurring genetic mutations. Therefore, using the current genetic tests, we can say to women, 'Yes, you are a carrier', or 'No, you are not', but there is a group of fifteen per cent surrounded by uncertainty, and it is an appalling predicament for them. Or what about the woman who is told, as a result of genetic screening, that there is a one-in-five possibility that her child will suffer from schizophrenia, perhaps, sometime. What anxieties would be hers? Could she cope? Would it be fair? Is it a sensible approach to human medicine?

These are some of the problems associated with the detection of genetic diseases. But that is only half the story. Genetic screening is only sensible and ethical if some form of treatment is available. Diagnosis without treatment is cruel medicine. So, what about treatments? There are already some proper ways of treating genetic diseases. For example, people with phenylketonuria, or a deficiency of the enzyme, lactase, can be given modified diets, that are restricted in phenylalanine and lactose, respectively. People who are deficient in a particular gene product can be supplied with it, so that those suffering from certain types of diabetes are given insulin, and those with haemophilia A are given factor VIII.

Future treatments will include genetic engineering in the form of gene therapy. This involves inserting a healthy gene into cells that carry a defective gene. Basically, there are two types. First, there is germline gene therapy, which inserts healthy genes into sperm, ova, or the gamete-producing cells. The effects would be heritable, therefore it is eugenic, and currently banned in the UK. Second, there is somatic gene therapy, which inserts healthy genes into specific cells, such as those of the liver, or skin. This is not heritable and is bioethically little different from transplants, like those of bone marrow, which are already widely accepted and used. In general, we need not fear properly-controlled somatic gene therapy. However, even here serious bioethical questions lie in wait. For example, should children be entitled to inherit unmanipulated genes? What about 'enhancement' experiments, inserting genes to improve physical, or mental, characteristics? When does 'enhancement' become 'treatment', and *vice versa*?

The basic protocol of somatic gene therapy is that the gene responsible for the disorder must first be identified, then isolated in its healthy form, then grown in large numbers, then transplanted. So far, the most successful strategy for somatic gene therapy uses viruses as the carriers, or vectors, to bring a particular DNA sequence, in the form of the healthy gene, into the 'defective' cells. But there are huge technical problems associated with packaging the DNA, targeting the right cells, and so on. Nevertheless, these procedures are currently being successfully used to treat patients with diseases such as severe combined immunodeficiency (SCID), hypercholesterolaemia, and cystic fibrosis, and these are bioethically unobjectionable procedures.

The first approved clinical trial of gene therapy started in the US in September 1990. The target was SCID. Sufferers have an impaired immune system and they have to live in sterile, plastic bubbles to protect themselves against potentially fatal infections. They have a faulty gene that does not code for a particular protein, the enzyme called, adenosine deaminase (ADA). So SCID patients are ADA-deficient. The first gene therapy patient was a four-year-old girl. Blood samples were taken from her and from these her T-lymphocyte cells were isolated, grown in a laboratory, and incubated with a viral vector containing the normal, healthy ADA gene. Then these cells were infused back into her bloodstream. Her condition improved, though she needed repeat treatments because the corrected T-cells died, so it was not a cure, but it was a watershed in gene therapy treatment.

Such is the huge potential for good that could come from genetic engineering. But genetics and genetic engineering are not everything. Some consider genetic engineering to be a threat to our humanness. Or some people harbour a fear that others will manipulate our genes and thus control our behaviour. These fears, quite unlike the others that have been raised in this book, are largely ungrounded. They presuppose that our genes determine entirely who we are, and how we will behave. But this, even if it were true, would mean, like all deterministic theories, that we would no longer be responsible for what we thought and did. Our limp excuse for sins, antisocial behaviour, and criminal activities would then be: 'My genes made me do it.' Thankfully, this cannot be true. Indeed, if it were true, it would run counter to the rugged insistence of the Bible's teaching that each human being is a free, moral agent, responsible before God for his, or her, own actions, thoughts, affections, and intents (Romans 3:19; 8:5-8; Ephesians 2:3; 4:17-19).

Furthermore, it cannot be true because we already know that our environment (commonly called 'nurture'), in addition to our genes ('nature'), plays a considerable part in our identity, that is, who we are, and how we behave. The beginnings of nurture, the genesis of the earliest times of human development from conception onwards, are quite different for each individual. This is why clones, though possessing identical biological 'natures', or genomes, would not be identical people. Even in the same womb, human clones would experience different micro-environments, and the complexities of their brain cell arrangements, like ours, would be quite unpredictable. Therefore we really are all different; each person, though made in the image and likeness of God, is unique, just as identical twins are, or even laboratory-produced human clones would be.

Yet, we are still more than mere products of our genetics and our environment, or of our 'nature' and 'nurture'. Even if we could fully describe a child's genes plus his environment we would never be able to predict the outcome of that child's life. To describe a person completely we must add what Baroness Warnock calls in her book, *An Intelligent Person's Guide to Ethics*, 'the human imagination', or, more fully and correctly, in the terminology of the Bible, the soul, or the interchangeable word, spirit.

Genetic engineering will never make a child more brave. Nor will it make a man more generous, or a woman more compassionate. Only God can bring about such permanent good in us. Why? Because God does not change our genes or environment, but rather our soul, our spirit (2 Corinthians 5:17; 1 Thessalonians 5:23).

3.6 Euthanasia

Some have considered euthanasia to be like the last in a row of three upended dominoes—once the other two had fallen, the third would inevitably follow. They have reasoned that once a society has accepted the practices of abortion (domino one) and infanticide (domino two), then why not domino three, euthanasia? After all, if we already abort our unborn and commit infanticide on our newborn because they are unwanted, or imperfect, or inconvenient, then why not euthanase the elderly and the unproductive?

Much of our uncertainty about euthanasia is because we are uncertain about death. Unlike most of us, the Bible tackles the subject of death, head-on. Indeed, it can be argued that there are only two topics throughout the whole Book, life and death. Death is thus a central theme of the Bible; one of its commonest phrases is: '... and he died'. Death is awesome for three reasons. First, death is awesome because it is the great inevitability (Job 14:5; Psalm 139:16). Our days are numbered—death will come to us all, one day. Second, death is awesome in its pervasiveness (Hebrews 9:27). Each year about 54 million people die world-wide. In the UK over 600,000 people die every year, leaving more than 1.5 million of us, as close family members, bereaved. Third, death is awesome because of its finality. Of course, earthly life is precious, but it must end (Isaiah 40:6-8; James 4:14; 1 Peter 1:24). Yet, 'Precious in the sight of the Lord is the death of his saints' (Psalm 116:15). When Christians die it is sad, but not a tragedy, rather it is the fulfilment of their salvation, a gateway to heaven.

But to die *well* is euthanasia. Yes, it is true. In the Middle Ages the terminally-ill were issued with booklets describing the *Ars Moriendi*—the art of dying well—to guide them through their last days and hours. You see, once upon a time, euthanasia (from the Greek, *eu*, well and *thanatos*, death) was a splendid word, something we could all aspire to. Now it has been hijacked and twisted, and turned into something ugly. Now it is associated with hovering doctors, pain, dehumanization, living wills, and bad decisions. It has become part of the culture of death.

Christians need to recapture the essence of true euthanasia. We have all begun the biological process of dying. Now we need to develop the spiritual process; we need a theology of living *and* of dying. Most of our days we resist death, but there will come a day when we must submit rather than resist. God will '... free those who all their lives were held in slavery by their fear of death' (Hebrews 2:15). Such a biblical perspective will deliver us, and those who care for us, from many of those potentially awful end-of-life decisions.

Therefore, we need to recognize, and clearly so, that there are times, especially as natural death comes very near, when medical treatment is futile and should be halted, otherwise it becomes 'meddlesome medicine'. At such times the doctor's intention is not to kill, but to provide the most comfortable environment, physically, mentally, and spiritually, in which the patient can die—this is *not* euthanasia. We also need to realize that, in a very real sense, doctors do, and always will, ultimately fail because every one of their patients will eventually die. That includes you, and me, and our nearest and dearest.

So what should we think of modern-day, so-called euthanasia? Our biblical, bioethical bedrock is this: we believe that it is God who sovereignly gives (Genesis 1:27; Acts 17:28), sustains (Psalm 66:9; Daniel 5:23; Hebrews 1:3), and finally takes life (Job 1:21; Ecclesiastes 8:8). Therefore we are opposed to modern euthanasia, whether it is carried out on the newborn (that is, infanticide) because of some genetic or physical disorder, whether the patient is elderly and judged to have a 'life not worthy to be lived', or whether it is defined in terms of deliberate acts, or deliberate omissions. If the intent is to kill the patient, it is euthanasia, and it is wrong. Such practices break the Sixth Commandment. Such procedures abrogate the historic role of the medical profession by ignoring the Hippocratic directive to 'Do no patient any harm'. Such actions are callous and unworthy of any decent society. So modern-day euthanasia must never be regarded as proper medical treatment. Killing the patient can never be the right answer.

The pro-euthanasia lobby often tries to distinguish between *active* (death caused by a deliberate act) and *passive* euthanasia (death caused by a deliberate omission, such as withholding or withdrawing treatment) by arguing that a patient who is deliberately starved to death is merely being *allowed* to die, rather than *caused* to die. But there is no moral difference between causing death by acts of omission, or causing death by deliberate acts—if the doctor's intention or aim is to shorten and end the patient's life, then it is euthanasia.

We need to be especially concerned about current, and future, pressures to legalize some forms of euthanasia. There is here a serious slippery slope—if *voluntary* euthanasia (that is, killing a patient on his request) is legalized, we will undoubtedly slip and slide into *non-voluntary* euthanasia (that is, killing a patient without an explicit request because it is assumed that it is in this person's best interests to be dead). Lastly, there is the horror of *involuntary* euthanasia (that is, killing a patient against his or her will, which is in effect the strong overruling the weak).

Evidence for the reality of this slippery slope is supplied by the famous Remmelink Report (1991), which reviewed 26,350 cases of 'medical decisions concerning the end of life' in Holland during 1990. It reported the occurrence of 2,300 cases of voluntary euthanasia and 400 cases of assisted suicide. But these were gross underestimates because the Dutch definition of euthanasia is restricted and includes only that which is active and voluntary. When passive and non-voluntary killings are included the Dutch data reveal that in 10,558 cases doctors had acted, or refrained from acting, with the 'explicit intention to shorten life', and that of these, 5,450 patients had been killed *without* their explicit request. In 1990 the total number of people who died in Holland was almost 130,000, therefore just over eight per cent of these deaths were as the result of euthanasia.

Matters will not improve for the Dutch people because, on 28 November 2000, their Parliament approved a Bill to legalize euthanasia. Thus, the Netherlands became the first country in the world to authorize this practice formally. Informally, euthanasia had long been tolerated in Holland, as it still is in other countries, such as Switzerland, Belgium, and Colombia. A few states have approved the practice of medically-assisted suicide, such as Oregon since 1994, as did the Northern Territory of Australia in 1996, though this was revoked by the federal Parliament the following year. Now the Dutch, including their children as young as sixteen, can opt for euthanasia. However, those aged between twelve and sixteen will first have to obtain the consent of one of their parents. Responding to this momentous shift in Dutch bioethics, the US-based Hemlock Society stated, 'We are very excited. We have admired what the people of Holland have been doing for the last twenty years.' Hmm!

Modern euthanasia has its origins firmly planted in the utilitarian worldview of human life. A 'life not worthy to be lived' is its benchmark. A lack of 'productivity' and 'usefulness' are its touchstones. 'Patient autonomy' is its yardstick. But it is always a shabby affair. In many cases it is nothing other than medically-assisted suicide—it is asking someone else, usually a doctor, to do the dirty work for us. How can this ever be called 'death with dignity'?

And if euthanasia were to be legalized in our society it would produce huge problems for us all. The elderly would feel a burden on their children and grandchildren. The daughter, who once upon a time gladly became a parent's lifelong carer, would feel that she had been cheated. The young family would start to begrudge the cost of long-term care as it whittled away the inheritance. Hints about the 'benefits' of voluntary euthanasia would become awkward table-talk. Sufferers of incurable illnesses, feeling depressed in those early days after diagnosis, might consider euthanasia to be attractive. And anyway, who might qualify for legalized euthanasia? It cannot be just those with incurable diseases. Some forms of asthma and arthritis, for example, are incurable, but no one is prescribing euthanasia for such sufferers. Nor could pain be the criterion, because many distressing illnesses, like quadriplegia and Parkinson's disease, are generally painless. So legalizing euthanasia would not usher in a problem-free era—far from it. On the other hand, we need to be realistic and entirely practical in this area. Nobody should underestimate the strains and tensions of caring for the sick and the elderly. There are inevitably huge problems which need to be tackled and shared, not shelved and ignored.

Other issues associated with modern-day euthanasia, such as, the use of 'quality of life' assessments and 'living wills' and 'advance directives' are troublesome. The former tends to be too subjective and hedonistic, while the latter are inappropriate and only serve to encourage a climate of medically-assisted suicide.

One major argument often raised in favour of euthanasia is centred on pain. We need to understand that the skilled use of analgesics has, by and large, eliminated pain as an issue in dying. The problem of pain undeniably exists, but the answer is not to legislate for euthanasia, but to commit more resources and care for those who are suffering. This is reinforced by a World Health Organization Expert Committee Report, *Cancer Pain Relief and Palliative Care* (1990), which states: '... with the development of modern methods of palliative care legislation of voluntary euthanasia is unnecessary. Now that a practical alternative to death in pain exists, there should be concentrated efforts to implement programmes of palliative care, rather than a yielding to pressure for legal euthanasia.' Medical treatment should always be provided when it will be beneficial to the patient, and palliative care when it will not, as admirably demonstrated by the hospice movement and its wonderful, pioneering work, particularly in the UK.

Just as easy abortion has created career difficulties for the morally-sensitive person in obstetrics and gynaecology, so euthanasia for the elderly, and infanticide for the newborn are having the same effect on those practising in geriatrics and paediatrics. These previously-honourable specialties are fast becoming part of the culture of death.

The pro-euthanasia lobby is usually appalled by comparisons made between it and the perpetrators of the Holocaust in Nazi Germany. For a scholarly, yet most unsettling account of the history of the latter, read

Michael Burleigh's *Death and Deliverance—'Euthanasia' in Germany 1900-1945*, and then judge for yourself.

Modern-day euthanasia cannot be fully understood without reference to the landmark legal case of Anthony Bland, the young victim of the Hillsborough disaster of 15 April 1989. He suffered severe brain damage and was later diagnosed as being in a persistent vegetative state (PVS). But contrary to popular belief, he was *not* on a life-support machine; his condition was fairly stable, he was able to breathe on his own, though he was fed artificially by tube. The judgement of the Law Lords on 4 February 1993, in the action of Airedale National Health Service Trust v. Bland, in effect, legalized euthanasia by omission.

The Law Lords stated that it would not be unlawful to withdraw treatment from Anthony Bland, so enabling him to die. The Law Lords said that Anthony Bland's life could be prematurely ended because 'treatment was futile' and 'invasive' and such a death was in 'his best interests' since he was 'a living death' with 'no dignity'. However, what caused, and still causes, the ethical uproar was that the so-called 'treatment' to be withdrawn was 'food and water'. In effect, he was dehydrated and starved to death over a nine-day period until he became the ninety-sixth Hillsborough victim. As Melanie Phillips (*The Guardian*, 5 February 1993, p. 20) perceptively observed, 'If it [nutrition] is treatment, then what precisely is the ailment for which food is the remedy?'

The Bland case opened the door, just a little. Since then the courts have sanctioned a steady stream of elderly patients, as well as those considered to be in a persistent vegetative state, to be 'allowed to die'. Euthanasia is undoubtedly coming in by the back door. Each court case opens the door a weeny bit more. At the turn of this century the British Medical Association issued new guidelines which permit doctors to withdraw food and water from such men, women, and children. And now there is a new fear on the wards. Some patients, without any discussion, and certainly not their consent, are having the frightening acronym, DNR (do not resuscitate) written on their hospital notes.

How far have we already slipped? How many more bioethical Rubicons are there to be crossed? Euthanasia is undoubtedly going to be a twenty-first century issue. How our society approaches it and responds to it will be a measure of our integrity and compassion. We do not need modern-day euthanasia—it is defeatist. We need to oppose every form of euthanasia and to encourage legislation, resources, and action that will support and cherish human physical, mental, and spiritual life, at all its stages.

The Christian gospel is the message of peace and hope. It proclaims that all human beings have the opportunity to be reconciled to their God (John 3:16; 6:40; Romans 5:10) and so live, and die, in peace and hope (Romans 5:1; Philippians 1:20-21; Hebrews 6:11). The people of God are entrusted with this gospel to demonstrate to all people how to live well, and how to die well. Christians must therefore be in the vanguard by showing principled compassion and practical care towards all those who suffer, including, of course, the dying.

3.7 Surrogacy

In terms of the culture of death, surrogacy is perhaps less mainstream. At least it seems a less barbarous practice since there is no primary intention to kill another human being. Nevertheless, it is still a sinister bioethical issue. The Warnock Report (p. 42) gave this definition: 'Surrogacy is the practice whereby one woman carries a child for another with the intention that the child should be handed over after birth.'

There are several variations on this theme, but the most common type of surrogacy is where a husband is fertile, but his wife is unable to sustain a pregnancy, possibly because of illness, or because she has had a hysterectomy. The hired surrogate woman is then inseminated, artificially or naturally, with the husband's sperm.

There are at least three surrounding topics to consider. First, we need, as always, to ask (and answer) some pretty fundamental questions, such as: Who are we? Are we simply cogs in a mechanistic universe? Is it right and proper to breed regardless of whose gametes are used? Does every woman (and man) have the right to have a child? Most of these questions have been addressed in the preceding pages.

Second, unfashionable as it may seem to be in some quarters, we cannot ignore the marriage covenant, this grand creational ordinance that has structured our societies and put us into families (Genesis 2:24; Psalm

68:6). It was given for our own good. Every human society has its roots in family life and only an obtuse few would argue that strong family life is bad for a society—even past and present UK governments would disagree with such an asinine proposition! Furthermore, the physical, procreative relationship is reserved for within the marriage covenant only (Matthew 19:4-6; Hebrews 13:4), and the intrusion of a third party, the surrogate, subverts this.

Third, children should be regarded as a precious inheritance, as gifts from God (Genesis 17:16; Psalm 127:3). The traditional biblical, and therefore the best, pattern is that children are conceived, born, and nurtured within the family unit. Even the authors of the Warnock Report (p. 11) recognized this: '... we believe that as a general rule it is better for children to be born into a two-parent family, with both father and mother ...'

So how does surrogacy measure up? It begins with an act of adultery. Some may argue that artificial insemination is only technical adultery. One of the earliest surrogate motherhood pacts was between Sarai, Abram, and Hagar (Genesis 16). This has been cited as a biblical justification for this old practice. It is no such thing! Verse 2 shows the frustrated Sarai seeking to overcome her infertility by using Hagar as a surrogate. It initially looked like a sensible, friendly agreement. But what followed was tension, separation, and broken relationships between all the parties concerned (Genesis 21:8-11), particularly the women (Genesis 16:4-6). It was a disaster.

If such an early surrogacy arrangement was problematic, then its modern-day counterparts are not without dilemmas too. There have been a sufficient number of freakish cases and human relationship minefields linked to surrogacy to make even its most ardent fans think again. Some cases are so outlandish that I have, from time to time, challenged others to sit around a table and construct the most preposterous surrogacy scenario we could think of—we have never come close to reality! Let me illustrate this with a recent notorious case, that of Claire Austin. She already had two daughters of her own, plus three from previous surrogate arrangements, one of which ended in abortion. But she wanted to try surrogacy, just one more time. The commissioning couple were an Italian man and a Portuguese woman, living in France. The sperm was obtained from a 50-year-old American, via a Danish sperm bank. The insemination procedure was carried out in Athens by a Greek doctor in February 1999. Twins were conceived. At twenty-one weeks of the pregnancy, the commissioning couple wanted to discover the twins' sex. When told that they were both girls they admitted that they wanted boys and asked Claire Austin to abort them. She refused and sought other commissioning parents over the Internet. Eventually, she was successful, and the twins went to live with a lesbian couple in Hollywood. Mrs Austin and that couple have since fallen out. She now says, 'Down with the cult of surrogacy!' She now says, 'Never again ... well, unless for a friend!' See what I mean? Weird, or what? Is not this the catastrophic actuality of 'babies as commodities'?

And there are additional tangled bioethical questions to ask. For example, if a married couple can hire a surrogate mother, why cannot a single woman, or a single man? Should a surrogate be allowed to, or made to, have an abortion? Should a surrogate child be allowed to know her genetic and her biological parents? Can the child inherit their property? What about surrogacy for a lesbian, or a transsexual, or a homosexual couple?

So what did the Warnock Report think of surrogacy? Tellingly, Warnock does not mention love, or deep affection, or emotion at this point, or for that matter, anywhere else. But in the midst of saying 'Yes' to virtually everything within its remit, the Warnock Report wanted surrogacy outlawed. It announced (p. 46), '... that surrogacy for convenience alone ... is totally ethically unacceptable.' Why such strong words? Is it not strange that, in the midst of so much permissiveness and uncertainty from the Warnock Report, it suddenly became so prohibitive and dogmatic? Apparently the members of the Warnock Committee were worried about money—if money changed hands then they thought that there must be some monkey business going on. The Committee was seemingly concerned (p. 46) about '... the danger of exploitation of one human being by another ...', that is, the use of *adults* (note, not the *children*) as a 'means to an end'. So commercial surrogacy was banned by a 1985 Act, and the Human Fertilisation and Embryology Act 1990 made commercial surrogacy arrangements legally unenforceable.

We may, for once, agree with the Warnock Report. But should we not go further? Should we view surrogacy not only as the commissioning mother wanting a child, but also as the surrogate, the natural mother (and in law, the legal mother) *not* wanting her child? The birth of any child is surrounded by a spectrum of emotions, perhaps none stronger than that of the mother's love for the child she has carried and delivered. Can a commissioning mother develop this latter love without the psychological and physical springs of this bonding, namely, pregnancy and childbirth?

Finally, the great difference here between surrogacy and adoption is that adoption seeks to enhance the love for, and security of, the child. Surrogacy has the long-term, premeditated intention for just the opposite. It is best avoided.

These are but outline notes on seven of the key bioethical issues. Read, mark, and learn them. As you add to your understanding you will be better equipped to resist the culture of death and to uphold the culture of life.

Some of the secondary issues

Responding to bioethical issues creates all sorts of tensions and problems for the Christian. When we read about the need for human embryo research to prevent human medical tragedies, are we not being hard-hearted to oppose it? When we hear the harrowing stories of the infertile, can you not begin to understand their hopes of IVF, or surrogacy? What about the stresses and strains of looking after senile parents, can you not see the need for euthanasia, at least, of the voluntary variety? Surely, some problem pregnancies would be better dealt with by abortion? Do you not feel a bioethical worm to be against all this? Well, we must learn to master our emotions and to handle these tensions. And the best, indeed the only, way forward is to increase our knowledge and understanding of these topics. Without such knowledge and understanding, we will be climbing onto an emotional rollercoaster—we will be tossed around like corks on the sea and our responses will be unsure and unhelpful. With such knowledge and understanding, our responses will be sure and helpful, because they will be rooted in principled compassion.

There are a dozen or so secondary, or peripheral, issues that can help us grasp these primary bioethical issues more firmly; they will bring them more clearly into context and focus. Additionally, they will help us better understand where others 'are coming from', and enable us to communicate with them, not only more knowledgeably, but also more cogently.

4.1 The need for ethical integration

This primer is about bioethical issues as they relate to human medicine. But such issues must not be neatly pigeonholed and segregated from other ethical issues that surround say, education, family life, or politics. We must not be 'one-issue' people. We must strive to be integrated people—never double-minded—with a consistent and robust ethical response to all of life's issues. This must be the aim of every Christian, to be mature, with the mind of Christ (1 Corinthians 2:16), informed by the Word of God (2 Timothy 3:16), and guided by the Holy Spirit (John 16:13).

4.2 Bioethical issues are for everyone

We must dismiss the idea that these bioethical issues are the sole preserve of the so-called experts, meaning, in particular, medical men and women. Such professionals obviously have considerable technical expertise, but they do not necessarily have any special bioethical insight—nor, of course, do we, unless we work at it! Truly, these issues are for us all. Sooner or later, we will all have to make big bioethical decisions. That will be when 'the rubber hits the road'—so now is the time to get a decent grounding and formulate a rugged and coherent biblical approach to these issues. Do not wait until you are confronted at the breakfast table, or across the doctor's desk, or at the hospital bedside.

4.3 A false view of bioethics

There is no doubt that Christians would like to ban, if not severely restrict, many practices within the culture of death. Some people will accuse us of wanting to impose our bioethical stance, sanctioned by the force of law. They fear the prospect of a Christian conviction imposed upon a pluralistic society. But this argument reflects a confusion about the relationship between law and ethics. A society's laws reflect that society's sense of justice and fairness and they therefore inevitably contain an ethical element. The ethically-neutral law is a myth. The question therefore is not whether laws should reflect an ethical worldview, but rather, *which* ethical worldview should they reflect? So why should the ethics of historic, orthodox, biblical Christianity be excluded from legal and public policy debates? If Christians do not speak up, others certainly will.

4.4 The importance of presuppositions

Everyone who comes to a bioethical debate comes with presuppositions; none comes empty-headed. These presuppositions are part of everyone's worldview, or frame of reference, that is, the means by which we decide what is right and what is wrong. These are picked up from parents, peers, papers, and so forth, and they are expressed in the language people use. We need to be aware and recognize this—it is everywhere, and it can be very subtle. For example, this very morning, I was on the radio pitted against the Director of the Nuffield Council on Bioethics, who was trying to defend the destruction of human embryos for therapeutic cloning on the grounds that they were 'only very early' embryos—as if the addition of two adverbs and an adjective somehow makes their extermination acceptable. Some scientists prefer to talk demeaningly about the pre-fourteen-day human embryo as a 'pre-embryo'. But, in deploring the coining of this new word, the *New Scientist* (21 November 1985, 108:17) forthrightly stated, 'Definitions are as important in science as the truth. Calling things by other names to suit the arguments will fool no-one.' So, is an abortion, a termination of a pregnancy (TOP), or the removal of the products of conception (POC), or the taking of the life of an unborn child? Is a human embryo a potential person, or a person with potential? It makes a world of difference.

We should also remember that a person's presuppositions will permeate and spill over into other bioethical issues. For example, a pro-abortionist is unlikely to have many qualms about destructive experimentation on human embryos. Similarly, someone already in favour of voluntary euthanasia could easily be persuaded of the merits of non-voluntary euthanasia.

We should also be able to recognize the presuppositional blindspots of others. For example, I have never understood why, on the one hand, the National Union of Students will campaign, quite rightly, against racism and ethnic cleansing, and will allow no discrimination against disabled people, and will even spend serious money on wheelchair access, and the like, for them. Yet, on the other hand, it will blindly give financial support to the National Abortion Campaign, which has consistently campaigned for the abortion of the disabled, up to birth. It is a clear case of bioethical duplicity.

4.5 Human value and worth

The question of human value and worth should not be a problem for the Christian, but it certainly is for the non-Christian. Today, men and women are commonly judged by how much they earn, or what they do for a living, rather than who they are, with their own intrinsic value and worth, simply because they are human beings and therefore made in the image of God.

Such vulgar assessments of people can be a serious problem; those who earn, or own, little, or who make little, or no, contribution to society are then often seen as a drag on society and as a burden to family and friends and therefore of no, or little, worth. And historically, people of limited value and worth have been considered to have 'lives not worthy to be lived', *lebensunwertes Leben*, the very maxim of the Nazi regime.

4.6 Consequences and principles

The terms 'pro-life' and 'pro-choice' are often employed as bioethical shorthand. They may at times be caricatures, but they are helpful here in denoting those who generally uphold the culture of life, and those who support the culture of death.

People's bioethical arguments and their decision-making are determined by their worldview. This leads to the concept of consequences and principles. For example, the arguments and decisions made by 'pro-choice' people are nearly always based upon consequences, which tend to emphasize a person's autonomy, that is, 'what is best for me'. Abortion is the great example. Here the typical consequence-based arguments are: 'I don't want it because I couldn't cope. Now is not a good time for me to be having a baby. My parents would throw me out if they knew.' The problem with this type of argument is that we are unable to control, or predict the consequences, so that any decision resting on consequences alone is inevitably built on shifting sand. For instance, a student, shocked at being told she is pregnant, requests an abortion because she feels isolated and without help and hope; the consequences of continuing with the pregnancy look too bleak. But, in the ensuing days, she may change her mind, especially if her friends, parents, university tutor, and father of the child rally round—that is, the predicted consequences, which formed the basis of her original decision, have changed.

On the other hand, the so-called 'pro-life' arguments and decision-making processes tend to be principle-based: 'It's wrong to take innocent human life. All euthanasia is bad medicine. Remember the Sixth Commandment.' Sometimes pro-life people can sound so principle-based that it seems as though they are not interested in the consequences to the woman and child, or to the disabled, or senile, person. Such an approach can be cold and cruel, cerebral and stand-offish. Moreover, it is certainly not the Christian response. When formulating arguments and making bioethical decisions, Christians should be concerned about both principles *and* consequences. Our responses must be rooted in principled compassion.

4.7 The meaning of autonomy

Autonomy (from the Greek, *autos*, self and *nomos*, law) means 'self-government' or 'personal freedom'. When properly applied this word can rightfully stress the moral responsibility that each of us should exercise. For example, medicine has recently seen a shift away from some of that awful medical paternalism of the past ('I'm the doctor, and I know what's best for you') towards a more reasonable patient autonomy ('But I'm the patient, so please explain it to me'). Such proper exercise of autonomy can only be beneficial to all concerned.

However, like several other good bioethical words, autonomy has now taken on a more malevolent meaning. As one of the catchwords of modern bioethics, it expresses the idea that we have the right to do whatever we want with our own lives, that there are no limits to our individual freedom. We can set our own rules and our own standards for morality and behaviour. This, of course, is nonsense. As members of society, we all accept certain boundaries to our freedom, such as observing speed limits, paying taxes, and keeping off the grass.

In the realm of bioethics, misapplied autonomy produces self-centred responses like: 'It's my body, it's my life, and it's my decision' and 'I will choose to die when and how I want to.' Such an overdose of autonomy can be disastrous. It allows the individual to take centre stage, to be the prima donna, or the leading man. So, for example, it excludes others from what would best be family-based, or even society-centred decisions. For instance, it can sideline friends, family, wise counsellors and, perhaps most importantly, the father, in the case of aborting the unborn child.

Autonomy, as a key feature of secular humanism and modern bioethics, puts the individual above all others, and it puts self, rather than God, at the centre. Think of all those unattractive, un-Christian words like, self-aggrandizement, self-assertion, self-centred, self-contained, self-indulgent, self-reliant, self-righteous, self-seeking, self-sufficient, and you will begin to understand both the meaning and the end product of modern autonomy.

4.8 The problem of rights

This leads to the subject of rights. And there are huge difficulties here for the Christian. The idea of rights originated from a European, liberal tradition some 800 years ago, rather than from the Bible and the Christian worldview. It began to blossom in the seventeenth century, and now 'rights-talk', 'rights-language' and 'rights-based morality' are common parlance in the students' union, the workplace, and among any who feel they have a grievance to be aired. Nowadays, everybody, everywhere is encouraged to 'claim their rights' and to 'get what is owed them'.

On 2 October 2000, the Human Rights Act came into effect. This was the UK's first written statement of people's rights. And sitting at the very top of the list of the seventeen rights, is, interestingly in the context of this book, 'the right to life'. Though what this actually means for human embryos, the unborn, the disabled, and the elderly has yet to be tested in our courts.

Even so, this human rights culture has already infiltrated many areas of bioethics, and the outcome has not been good. A woman may talk about insisting upon *her* rights, but subtly the dynamics of such insistence often conceal the fact that she is actually making claims upon others. She may consider it is her 'right' to have a child, so she claims this from her doctor—he must arrange IVF treatment for her. Similarly, a doctor must arrange an abortion for another woman, because that is her 'right'. Or, because the old man thinks he has a 'right' to die, his doctor must participate in his medically-assisted suicide.

All this talk of rights creates additional problems for the thinking Christian. What is the origin of these rights—are they given by God, or by society, or by self? What are their limits—are they personal and ephemeral, or are they universal and permanent? What is their hierarchy—is the right to work superseded by the right to life? Are a mother's rights greater than her unborn child's? Who decides when there is a conflict of rights—is it the patient, or the family, or the doctor, or the courts?

The Scriptures take a quite different tack. They stress our responsibilities rather than our rights. The Christian mind has a well-developed sense of gratitude. Christians know that they are debtors, that they are owed nothing, and that all they are, and all they possess, has been given by the grace of God alone (Psalm 130:3-4; Ephesians 2:8). So a Christian will not be 'on the take', but 'on the give'. A Christian will major on his responsibilities, his duties, his obligations, not on his rights. Was it the robbed and beaten man's right to be helped, or was it the good Samaritan's responsibility to assist him (Luke 10:25-37)? Was it Paul's right to expect the hospitality of Gaius, or was it Gaius' happy duty to look after the apostle (Romans 16:23)? I think you know.

4.9 The nature of dependency

Mutual dependency is a Christian characteristic. Yet some people despise such a notion. For example, proponents of euthanasia consider that dependency is degrading and dehumanizing. 'People', they say, 'should be free to live and to die. They should be totally free to decide for themselves. They should be wholly independent.' But such stark independency is the ugly sister of autonomy. The young rebel longs to be free; no limits, no rules, no parents, no nothing—totally independent and totally autonomous.

On the other hand, as John Donne famously wrote in his *Meditation XVII*, 'No man is an Island, entire of it self', and more appositely Paul wrote in Romans 14:7, 'For none of us lives to himself alone and none of us dies to himself alone.' So dependency is a feature of proper living, not only dependency upon God, but also dependency upon others within a community. Christians, above all others, should be living in mutual interdependency (Romans 12:4-5; 1 Peter 2:4-10) and perhaps we need to recover and reaffirm this theme. Such a recovery would counter the sterile individualism of much of our society, with its overemphasis on personal autonomy and rights. For the Christian, it is the Church, the body of Christ, that is the working model (Romans 12:4-8; 1 Corinthians 12:12-31), and the Bible, the Word of Christ, that is the blueprint, the maker's handbook, the master plan.

4.10 Changing views of the medical profession

We have already noted the rapid changes that have occurred in medical ethics and practice during the last fifty or so years. Alongside these have been changes in the way we, the general public, perceive the medical profession. Nowadays, doctors are less likely to be those old-fashioned carers and healers, who knew all about us and our families. Instead, they are more likely to be modern resource-allocators, often far removed from that original Hippocratic type of patient-doctor relationship.

Furthermore, we now tend to perceive and treat doctors as 'need-meeters'—we ask, and they give. You are pregnant and do not want to be, so you go along to your doctor and say, 'Please meet my need.' You are infertile and you say, 'Please meet my need.' Your life is miserable and you say, 'Please meet my need.'

More and more doctors are becoming mere public servants, doing what other people tell them to do, rather than abiding by the original ideals of their profession. Of course, this new perception of the medical profession is especially unnerving within the culture of death. Here doctors are no longer healers and preservers, but rather takers and dispatchers of human life. They are the social executioners of our time. We approve abortion—they do it. We want infanticide—they carry it out. We legalize euthanasia—they execute it.

4.11 Financial resources and medicine

Medicine costs money, and economics influences the practice of medicine. There is always a finite pot of cash and not every procedure, operation, or drug regime can be afforded. In other words, there has to be some rationing, as it used to be called, or as it is now known, resource allocation, and what will, in the near future, be termed, sustainability. Whatever it is called, its implementation should be honest and equitable—the poor, the small, and the vulnerable must not be discounted or sidelined.

Our society tends to make more and more judgements based on economic criteria and people's perceived value and worth, but such thinking and practice must be resisted. To this end, the increasing involvement of Christians in costly initiatives, such as homes for the mentally handicapped, practical care and accommodation for pregnant women and girls, respite care for carers, and the hospice movement, is to be warmly welcomed and encouraged. But more is needed—the State cannot, or will not, ever provide enough.

4.12 The changing role of the law

Parallel to these changes in medicine have been changes in the law. What has happened with abortion law is very instructive. Our abortion law was changed radically in 1967. The new law gave permission for abortion to be performed under certain, limited circumstances. But that original *permission* soon became an *expectation*. Any woman attending an abortion clinic expected to be given an abortion. But that expectation has now become a *requirement*. In the current climate of 'abortion-on-demand', or the 'free supply of abortion', a woman no longer simply expects, but now actually requires, an abortion. Can you see the reality of the legal slippery slope? Think how this might affect for example, euthanasia legislation. The legal boundaries in these matters of life and death need to be much more carefully and tightly drawn—loopholes have a nasty habit of getting stretched, and sometimes they even break.

4.13 The slippery slope

This brings us to what some bioethicists call the 'thin end of the wedge', the 'opening of the door', the 'domino effect', and other such phrases. Whatever it is called, the idea is simple: once a previously unthinkable practice has been legalized, that practice inevitably grows in public acceptability, and it also grows numerically. There are two main causes of this phenomenon. First, the very basis of most Acts of Parliament, or government regulations, is arbitrary. They reflect the lack of any firm bioethical foundation. They often contain vague words like 'substantial' and 'normally'. These produce confusion, which allows interpretation, which encourages, not just a moving, but also a widening of the goalposts. Second, the very practice itself will throw up 'difficult' or 'hard' cases. These go through the courts, which make new case law, which also expands the original legal goalposts. Yes, the old aphorism is true: 'hard cases make bad law'. The death of a few, be they embryos, foetuses, unborn children, or the elderly, will inevitably become the death of many.

The wedge will penetrate deeper and deeper, the door will slowly open wider and wider. The once unthinkable will soon become acceptable, the once limited will soon become widespread.

Just three examples should suffice to demonstrate the reality of the slippery slope. First, you see it numerically, with abortion. In 1966, there were 6,100 recorded abortions in NHS hospitals. The next year, one year after the infamous Act, the slippery slope had started and there were 23,641 abortions in England and Wales. A mere six years later we were slipping down the slope helter-skelter and there were 162,941 abortions; an almost seven-fold increase. The steepness of this slope took even the pro-abortion Parliamentarians quite by surprise.

Second, you see it in broken promises, with the 'post-coital', or the 'morning-after', pill. This high dose of progestogen, with its abortifacient activity, was introduced into the UK in the 1980s, amid protests from many pro-life people, but with reassurances from the Department of Health and Social Security that it would be used only in exceptional circumstances, and that it would remain as a prescription-only drug. At the end of 2000, the government approved it for over-the-counter sales at chemists' shops to girls over sixteen. By the beginning of 2001, it was available for under-age girls from nurses in selected state schools. No longer will doctors supervise its use and no longer will it be regarded as 'emergency-only contraception'—street-wise girls will carry it in their handbags as an 'ever-ready' aid. The once-tight regulations have been relaxed—we are now well on the slippery slope. What next? Will 'morning-after' pills be available at all good supermarkets and petrol stations? Will they be included in every student's welcome pack on their first day at secondary school?

Third, you see it in society's thinking, with regard to the disabled. We have already described the 'search-and-destroy' armoury, namely, the well-established prenatal diagnosis plus abortion, and the relatively new procedure of preimplantation genetic diagnosis. The political, medical, and social mindsets have been formulated—most disabled people have 'lives not worthy to be lived'. Therefore we should do our best to get rid of them, but, of course, as early as possible, and preferably before they make their presence felt, or seen. So both bioethical feet are firmly on the slope.

The full spectrum of destruction of the disabled is now available. It begins with destroying the disabled as preimplanted embryos, then it descends to aborting the unborn, finally there is a rapid descent that ends with the deaths of the newborn, in infanticide.

But some disagree. They see no slippery slopes, dominoes, doors, or wedges. The case of R v. Arthur was perhaps the most famous infanticide trial of the last century. In 1980, Dr Leonard Arthur had prescribed dihydrocodeine and 'nursing care only' to John Pearson, a newborn infant with Down's syndrome, who died four days later. Dr Arthur was charged with attempted murder, but on 5 November 1981, he was acquitted. It was a most controversial verdict. The doyen of bioethical law, Professor Ian Kennedy of London University, wrote an article in *New Society* (7 January 1982, pp. 13-15) entitled, 'Reflections on the Arthur Trial'. He concluded, 'I am not persuaded of the inevitability of the wedge argument—that one step down the road towards removing one class of the disabled, the very severely disabled child, from our midst—means that we must inevitably take the next step.' Professor Kennedy does not appear to understand bioethical history, or human nature. Or maybe both.

Baroness Warnock, perhaps not surprisingly, also has contempt for the slippery slope argument. She maintains in her book, *An Intelligent Person's Guide to Ethics* (p. 37) that it is 'an illogical argument' which is '... used by people who do not trust doctors or hospital ethics committees.' Well, you are partly right there, Mrs Warnock!

These dozen or so secondary issues will lie in ambush, lurking in the background of any discussion of bioethical issues. Understand them and you will be better equipped to meet the day, as well as the opposition.

When does human life begin?

The most commonly-asked question in bioethics is: When does human life begin? The answer you give indicates your views on practically every bioethical issue. It will reveal your thinking on the biological, legal, and sociological status of the human embryo, your regard for the human foetus, and how you would treat the unborn child. But there is much more at stake here than revealing just one person's worldview. This great question also has a collective, a societal answer. And with that answer comes the implicit understanding of when 'it' is worthy of some respect, and when 'it' is to be protected by the laws of that society. So the question is pointed—it has both a private and a public dimension— and the answer is pivotal—it either opens, or closes the door to the culture of death.

So, because of its crucial nature in bioethics a whole chapter will be devoted to a discussion of this question. True, we have already considered the biblical evidence in section 2.2. For many that is sufficient—and quite right too! But that is not the end of the matter. For if we are going to speak out there, in the so-called real world, then we would be wise to be well-acquainted with the arguments of others. We should never be afraid to tackle the world and its thinking—the Christian-based, pro-life case is unanswerable. Why should we fear truth?

Basically, there are four schools of thought, and therefore four answers to this great question.

5.1 The lazy school

The answer from this school is: 'I don't know, and don't care.' This is rarely encountered, though some of my (less successful) students have been known to hold this indolent view—I trust no reader does.

5.2 The agnostic school

The second answer given is: 'It is unanswerable, the question is too difficult.' This is bioethical agnosticism. Some from this school will mock anyone who has the audacity even to ask such a foolish question—they will chide the questioner for being simplistic. Others will prefer to shelter behind the semantics of psychobabble, so they will talk somewhat arrogantly, or perhaps mystically, of the importance of 'personhood' and 'ensoulment', neither of which they can define adequately. But the question is much more straightforward than either of these two red herrings imply—do not let the blatherskites hide behind these sophistic smokescreens!

Nevertheless, there are some sensible bioethical agnostics, who are genuinely uncertain about an answer. To be consistent and true to themselves, those who hold such a view, must take a very conservative stance over this question and provide protection for all human life from the earliest times, otherwise they run the risk of killing, or abusing a fellow human being. If you are not sure, then you are extremely careful. That is, you err on the side of caution. The famous analogy is that of the mountain rescue team, which decides not to venture out on a cold and frosty night because there is at least an even chance that the lost climbers will be already dead—no decent rescue team would think and behave like that. So likewise, bioethical agnostics must be extra-circumspect—genuine bioethical agnosticism is therefore incompatible with destructive human embryo experimentation, abortion, and so on.

5.3 The gradualist school

The third answer comes from those who belong to the gradualist school. They admit that the developing embryo, or foetus is becoming 'one of us', but they maintain that some observable trait, some recognizable feature has to arrive, or be reached before the 'it' has truly become 'one of us'. Initially, this may hold some attraction. All of us know of the greater expectancy as a pregnancy continues and the unborn child develops. Bonding and excitement increase when we see the first ultrasound pictures, or feel the first kicks. But can one criterion of recognition, or the appearance of one physical feature, selected from among the myriad of contemporaneously occurring developmental changes, be sufficient to define that momentous watershed, namely, the beginning of human life? And, if it were so, what about one day, or one hour, or one minute *before* that criterion was recognized? Philosophically, that would seem to be an implacable objection to the gradualist's position. But read on.

This gradualist school is a mixed school—it has several classes—six will be examined here.

5.3.1 After birth

The first answer is a seemingly outrageous possibility—sometime after birth. Its proponents say that the newborn is not really 'one of us' until as much as one year after birth, when the activity of the brain has developed so that the powers of speech and communication have begun. Amazingly, the two Nobel prize-winners, who discovered the structure of DNA, support this general view. One is James Watson, who has said, 'If a child were not declared alive until three days after birth, then all parents could be allowed the choice only a few are given under the present system' (*Prism*, May 1973, 1:13). Watson is thus also a proponent of infanticide. Similarly, his Nobel prize collaborator, Francis Crick has said, '... no newborn infant should be declared human until it has passed certain tests regarding its genetic endowment and that if it fails these tests, it forfeits the right to live' (quoted by the *Pacific News Service*, January 1978). This is frightening stuff from the elite of the biological sciences.

5.3.2 At birth

This second criterion is still popular with the great British public as the indicator of the beginning of human life. True, it is a very dramatic step. For the first time in nine months we can properly see, hear, touch, taste, and smell the baby. Oh yes, birth is an emotional time—I've been there! Birth also heralds a new independence for the baby, though self-sufficiency is still many years away. Birth is also the beginning of lung breathing and oral feeding, but the objects of breathing and feeding, namely, respiration and nutrient supply, have been occurring since when? Well, every living cell, including that tiny zygote, must respire and receive nutrients. These two biological processes are part and parcel of all life, so at birth they cannot be diagnostic of life's beginning because they have been going on already for the previous nine months or so. It is simply the mode of breathing and feeding that changes at birth.

Incidentally, it is a false exegesis of Genesis 2:7: 'And the Lord God ...

breathed into his (Adam's) nostrils the breath of life ... ', to conclude that 'breath' and 'life' are in some way uniquely cause-and-effect, and therefore mark the beginning of every human being's existence. The 'breath of life' was common to every living creature (Genesis 6:17). But the creational event recorded in Genesis 2 occurred once only, when God transformed the dust of the ground into a living being. Therefore Adam was quite different from us in this respect; he had no conception, no nine-month gestation, no belly button! Verses, such as Job 33:4 and Acts 17:25, simply emphasize our Adamic lineage and our dependence upon the sustaining power of God. They lend no credence to the idea that our first extra-uterine breath marks the beginning of our life.

5.3.3 Viability

The third gradualist school's possibility is that human life begins at viability, when the child can survive outside the womb. The law in England and Wales, in the form of the Infant Life (Preservation) Act 1929, has protected unborn children once they are 'capable of being born alive'. But when is this viability attained? In the UK, at least in 1929 and for sometime after, it was understood to occur at twenty-eight weeks. But it has been constantly decreasing with advances in obstetric practice. Nowadays, premature babies of a gestational age of twenty-three, or even twenty-two weeks survive. So viability is a changing definition and therefore unsatisfactory as a criterion to provide the unborn with either that certain status which engenders legal protection, or for the parents to declare, 'Look, our child's life has just begun.' Viability is, in a word, insufficient.

5.3.4 Some indicator

The fourth answer given depends upon the appearance of various indicators. For example, some consider that the appearance of blood, at about three weeks into the pregnancy, is significant. This criterion has even been used with supposedly biblical warrant. Again, this is faulty exegesis, in this case of Genesis 9:4: 'But you must not eat meat that has its lifeblood still in it.' This, and other similar Mosaic passages, are chiefly concerned with God granting his people animal flesh to eat. Moses uses 'blood' tautologically to expound 'life', in much the same way that the New

International Version of the Bible uses the single word, 'lifeblood'. Calvin agrees, and commentates (*Genesis*, Banner of Truth, 1965, p. 293): '... not because blood is in itself the life but ... a token which represents life.' In other words, it is a colloquial device. What Moses is doing here is cautioning the people of Israel to view and handle blood with respect and care, since it was, and still is, the means of atonement. This theme of the blood finds fruition in John 6:53-56. It has nothing to do with defining the beginning of human life.

Others choose as their criterion the appearance of brain waves, at about six weeks, sometimes referred to as sentience, that is, when the unborn child reacts with the environment, has the capacity to feel sensation, and responds to stimuli. For example, the influential Australian bioethicist, Peter Singer and Deane Wells, an Australian politician, have argued the case in their book, *The Reproduction Revolution* (Oxford University Press, 1984), for brain function (p. 98): 'We suggest that the embryo be regarded as a thing, rather than a person, until the point at which there is some brain function. Brain function could not occur before the end of the sixth week after conception.' But this, like all other such indicators, are simply expressions of processes already going on, and proceeding at tremendous rates. In addition, they all depend upon the sensitivity of the technology used to detect them. If we take the 'appearance of blood' as 'the beginning', then what is the measure? Is it when blood is first visible with a naked eye, or with a light microscope, or an electron microscope, or is it when the blood vessels are being structured, or when the blood proteins are being synthesized? We have here a process, or rather, a series of processes, by which blood appears. Therefore, if this is the answer to the big question, it is inevitably going to be 'about so many days'. That is, it is going to be non-specific, imprecise, and therefore unsatisfactory.

5.3.5 Primitive streak

Fifth, there is the Warnock Report's favourite, the appearance of the primitive streak, at about day fourteen. The Warnock Report was concerned to produce a recommendation for an upper time limit for experimenting on human embryos. In other words, it set a time limit *after* which it presumed there was something valuable present, something to be protected, but *before* that time limit there was something of lesser value that could be freely experimented upon, and indeed, capriciously destroyed. So, by default, the Warnock Committee was defining the beginning of human life, or, at least, a stage, which the Committee members considered to be sufficiently significant, after which the embryo commanded some respect by experimenters, as well as some protection by the law.

The Warnock Report (p. 59) decided that the primitive streak was definitive because it is, '... a heaping-up of cells at one end of the embryonic disc on the fourteenth or fifteenth day after fertilisation.' By contrast, major scientific authorities, such as Leon W Browder (*Developmental Biology*, Saunders College, Philadelphia, 1984, 2nd edition, pp. 609, 615) consider that the primitive streak is merely, '... a passageway through which cells of the embryo pass in order to continue differentiation.' Nothing much definitive about that, is there?

One question worth asking is: Why fourteen days? Why not seven, or twenty-one days? Why not indeed? One French research group suggested twelve weeks, which was the legal deadline for abortions in France. That, at least, possesses a certain logic—why should the killing of embryos have a different timetable from the killing of foetuses? So why fourteen days? Strangely, and almost incredulously, Warnock (p. 65) states, '... once the process has begun, there is no particular part of the developmental process that is more important than another; all are part of a continuous process ...' And the Report continues (p. 65), 'Thus biologically there is no one single identifiable stage in the development of the embryo beyond which the in vitro embryo should not be kept alive.' So, according to the Warnock Report, there is no scientific justification for choosing a cut-off point. You would therefore expect none to be proposed. But the Warnock Report proposes fourteen days. In view of the above, is this not intellectually indefensible?

But Warnock (p. 65) says, '... some precise decision must be taken ...' 'Why?', you may ask. Warnock answers, '... in order to allay public anxiety.' So, though this is admittedly absurd and arbitrary, fourteen days will keep the public happy, even though it is pulling the wool over our eyes. So the Warnock Report forgets what has gone before and decides that there really is a stage, a time when something of value is present, beyond which we should not go, namely, when the primitive streak appears.

In an attempt to reinforce this arbitrary significance of the primitive streak, the Warnock Report produces two arguments. First, the Report maintains that it is the earliest recognizable feature of the embryo proper (p. 59), 'The primitive streak is the first of several identifiable features ...' However, it is certainly not the beginning of differentiation because at the morula stage (about day three and sixteen cells), cells of the so-called inner mass are distinguishable. Moreover, at the early blastocyst stage (about day six), the inner mass cells have separated from those of the trophoblast, the outer layer from which the placenta and other tissues develop. So this ephemeral appearance of the primitive streak is but one of many, many events that take place in the early days and weeks of a human life.

The second argument Warnock (p. 59) produces says, 'This is the latest stage at which identical twins can occur.' The Report's idea is that embryo experimentation should not occur after twinning because we would then certainly be dealing with human individuals. So, it is permissible to keep an embryo alive until then, but wrong afterwards. This is philosophical bromide, for at least four reasons. First, if this is true, then the ban on experimentation should be at the earliest, not the latest, that twinning could occur—identical twins can arise at the two-cell stage on day one, or day two. Second, the 'trigger', or the determinant, for twinning may occur at fertilization. Our understanding of the twinning process is poor, so what is more correct to say is, that twinning is observable later on, not that it necessarily commences later on. Third, if twinning does occur at some time subsequent to fertilization, what do we conclude? Now there are two individuals, two embryonic human beings. But before that, what was there? There was not none. There was always at least one. Fourth, if experimentation is objectionable on post-fourteen-day individuals, and since it is impossible to spot the minority of potential 'twinners' in advance, then should not all embryo experimentation be halted?

The primitive streak fails as a criterion for the beginning of human life, or, for that matter, for anything else of much significance. And thus the fourteen-day rule is shown for what it really is, humbug.

5.3.6 Implantation

The sixth answer sometimes given is, implantation. This has become popular since the 1980s, when the Department of Health and Social Security (DHSS) re-wrote basic human biology, as once we all knew it, and invented the 'new biology'. This is another example of lexical engineering preceding social engineering—an important, but reprehensible feature of much of modern bioethics. Mass abortion has already been subsumed under the seemingly respectable guise of 'termination of pregnancy,' 'removal of the products of conception', or 'a woman's right to choose'. Now a similar verbal cloak is being used to cover up the truth about the beginning of human life. We should not be fooled.

Implantation occurs about six days after fertilization and lasts for between five and twelve days. It is therefore a process that lasts about a week. Advocates of the 'new biology' claim that conception and fertilization are now *not* the same. This flies in the face of centuries of biological scholarship. Nevertheless, they now say that conception has not taken place until implantation of the embryo in the mother's womb has occurred. So a pregnancy does not now last on average forty weeks, but only thirty-nine weeks and one day. *Ipso facto*, human life begins at day six, or thereabouts.

Despite the fact that the embryo is carried by the mother before implantation, they now say that 'carriage' does not begin until implantation. In defiance of common sense, they say something cannot be carried unless it is actually attached to the person. But what about the pound coin in my pocket? This 'new biology' was a mischievous invention by the DHSS to ensure that the post-coital (or 'morning-after') pill was no longer illegal. It operates as an abortifacient, rather than as a contraceptive, so its use would have contravened the Offences Against the Person Act 1861, which forbids the 'procuring of a miscarriage'. The age-old definition of the word 'contraception', from its Latin roots (*contra*, against and *conceptum*, conception), has clearly meant keeping sperm and ova apart, by either physical, or chemical means to prevent conception, or fertilization. This 'new biology' now demands a different definition. Now contraception is the use of something that works up to six days after fertilization, something that can destroy the human blastocyst, prior to implantation.

Some of these gradualists' steps and stages in the fabulous early development of a human being are undoubtedly huge, but is any sufficient to count convincingly as *the* beginning of human life? Can we say with conviction of any of them: 'Before this I was not—now I am'?

5.4 The conception school

The fourth and final school says that human life begins at the earliest time point, namely, conception, or fertilization. This was certainly the view expressed in the Declaration of Geneva 1948: '... from the time of conception ...' It is also the standard opinion of all the leading medical and biological textbooks published throughout most of the twentieth century.

What happens at fertilization, or conception? Once a month, a woman normally ovulates, that is, she produces an ovum, some 140 μm in diameter. This begins a journey down one of the Fallopian tubes to the uterus. If sexual intercourse occurs, some 300 million sperm, each about 50 μm in length, are deposited in the vagina and begin a journey towards the Fallopian tubes. For conception to occur, one sperm must penetrate the ovum. The head of the successful sperm absorbs fluid from the ovum and forms a spherical nucleus. The two nuclei approach one another and fuse to produce a fertilized ovum, called a zygote. This is THE BEGINNING.

Some have confusingly thought that if fertilization marks the beginning of human life, then why cannot the zygote's precursors, the sperm and ovum, be regarded as the beginning too? After all, they are human. That is incontestable. And they are alive. True, they are alive, but they are unable to replicate, or reproduce, or genetically express themselves. They will die rapidly unless they are kept alive artificially. Whatever, they will be forever only single cells. But, when one fuses with the other, twenty-three chromosomes from the mother's ovum and twenty-three chromosomes from the father's sperm produce a new, genetically unique, human being. This zygote contains all the hereditary material, the forty-six chromosomes, for the future girl or boy, woman or man. From this zygote, this one cell, will develop all the different organs, tissues, and features of the human body. Is there anything more commonplace, yet more amazing?

Once fertilization has occurred, the first cell division (mitosis) takes place after about thirty hours. After about three days there is an embryo of approximately sixteen cells, a small ball, called a morula. After about six days, the embryo, now called a blastocyst, reaches the uterus. It is here that implantation occurs. Enzymes from the embryo produce a small cavity in the receptive uterine wall, or endometrium, and the embryo adheres there. Around day ten, fingerlike projections penetrate the wall and the embryo begins absorbing nutrients from the mother's blood supply. Hormonal changes alter the monthly cycle so that the uterine lining is not shed at fourteen days after ovulation. At this stage, the embryo is about 1.5 mm in length and the mother misses her period and suspects she is pregnant. From weeks two to four there is a rapid and amazing differentiation into eyes, brain, spinal cord, lungs, digestive system, and the heart, which starts beating at about day twenty-one. And so this growth and development continues for about another eight months, until birth.

From all the potential permutations of all my father's sperm and all my mother's ova, the uniting of just two produced ME. That is where and when I began. We were all once a zygote, a morula, a blastocyst, an embryo. Once fertilization had occurred, all these other events were set in motion. Implantation, viability, birth, infancy, teenage years, adulthood—these are simply stages in a human life already begun.

Why have I laboured this? Because when we read the Warnock Report, scientific research papers, IVF clinic leaflets, and when we hear news and discussions on television and radio, we are presented with information and opinions about zygotes, and blastocysts, and human embryos. Similarly, when we discuss abortion, we are confronted with terms like foetus, the products of conception, and the unborn child. And we need to decide what we (and others) are talking about. Are we talking about human lives and fellow human beings? Are we dealing with 'one of us', or are we dealing with something else? And, if so, then what is it. We need to know.

So when does human life begin? Think carefully before you give your reply. Your answer to this question is crucial in expressing your views on, and formulating your responses to, the whole range of bioethical issues.

How did we get the 1967 Abortion Act?

Contrary to the schoolboy's paraphrase of Hegel's dictum, history *can* teach us something. Looking back and seeing how these issues developed will help us understand more fully why we are in the bioethical mess, in the culture of death, we are today. Changes in abortion law provide an excellent vehicle to demonstrate how that potent mix of a nation's ethical decline, the ambitions of an elite few, the communication of some half-truths, a distracted church, and some political shenanigans can alter our world, for the worse.

Though the changes outlined here applied specifically to the case of England, Wales, and Scotland (the 1967 Act does not extend to Northern Ireland), the themes have been similar for Western countries in general. Moreover, these changes in abortion law heralded significant alterations with regard to other bioethical issues too. That is, they prefigured many subsequent agendas and they also set the pattern for perpetrating them. Such historical perspectives are not only fascinating, they are also instructive—the lessons of bioethical history are there to be learned. And they may help us to avoid making the same mistakes again, *Deo volente*.

6.1 Pre-1967 abortion laws

Abortion has doubtless occurred throughout history and in all cultures. While it is still illegal in almost all countries of the world, it is also now generally permissible, under certain circumstances.

It seems that from the times of the Saxons, and certainly from the thirteenth-century, according to Henry de Bracton, an authoritative writer on English law from that period, it was the accepted legal opinion that to kill a foetus which was 'formed or animated' in the womb was murder, or at least, manslaughter. However, during those times, the definitions of, and associated punishments for, abortions were often variable and were generally a matter for the ecclesiastical courts. The latter were abolished during the Reformation and the crime of abortion became the province of the Common Law courts. In the seventeenth century, Lord Coke and others redefined murder as the unlawful killing of a 'reasonable creature in being', or in *rerum natura*, that is, one living *outside* the womb. Even so, to kill an unborn child, that is, one living *inside* the womb, 'once its presence was made known', though no longer regarded as murder, remained a serious criminal offence. Then came Lord Ellenborough's 1803 Act, which made abortion a statutory, or in the word of the Act, a 'heinous', offence. It further unambiguously stated that, '... in every such case the Person or Persons so offending, their Counsellors, Aiders, and Abettors, knowing of and privy to such Offence ... shall suffer Death.' Thus, Parliament declared that the abortion of a 'quick foetus', that is, one capable of extensive and felt movements, at about sixteen to eighteen weeks onwards, was a capital offence. Even when abortions were performed at 'pre-quickening', that is before sixteen weeks, they were still a criminal offence, though there were lesser penalties, like fines, imprisonment, whipping, or transportation, for those performing them.

There were other pieces of legislation, such as Lord Lansdowne's Act 1828 and the Offences Against the Person Act 1837, which made minor changes to our abortion law. But it was the wide-ranging Offences Against the Person Act 1861, which brought together several aspects of legal protection for the individual (from making gunpowder to interrupting church services) that was to become the long-standing abortion benchmark. Sections 58 and 59 outlawed abortions and made it a crime for a pregnant woman, or anyone else, to attempt, or assist by '... poison, or any noxious thing, or ... any instrument or other means whatsoever ...' '... to procure the miscarriage of any woman ...', even if the woman was not pregnant. The maximum penalty was life imprisonment.

The Infant Life (Preservation) Act 1929 then filled a gap in the law by protecting the unborn child who might be killed during the course of actually being born. The Act stated that a woman who had been '... pregnant for a period of 28 weeks or more shall be *prima facie* proof that she was at that time pregnant of a child capable of being born alive'. The crucial phrase was a child 'capable of being born alive'. It did not say that a child of less than twenty-eight weeks is *not* capable of being born alive, nor did it deal with subsequent survival. This twenty-eight-week cut-off may have been acceptable as the lower time limit of survival some seventy years ago, but it is well-known that modern neonatal care allows those of twenty-six, twenty-four, or even twenty-two weeks not only to be born alive, but also to survive. It should also be noted that neither the 1861, nor the 1929, Acts say that an offence has been committed if the pregnancy is terminated '... for the purpose only of preserving the life of the mother'.

So, what were the reasons for the radical reform of these abortion laws during the 1960s? How did England, Wales, and Scotland come to acquire just about the earliest and the worst abortion law in Europe, the West, and even the world? How did we get the 1967 Abortion Act? It seems that there are at least ten reasons.

6.2 The social revolution

The Swinging Sixties were times of unparalleled social upheaval. It was the time of the coming-of-age of the post-war children. Public morality was in a trough. There was a new affluence, an emerging feminist movement, freely-available drugs, and increasing sexual promiscuity—a social revolution was underway, and the world would never be the same again. It was also a time when the church was in general disarray and decline. Much of it was becoming an insipid reflection of society—the liberals were in charge and they had hopelessly lost their way. Just think, the most influential Christian book of the 1960s was Bishop John Robinson's *Honest to God*, which was a sceptical diatribe against historic, biblical Christianity—thankfully, no one bothers to read it today! So, the time was ripe for the liberalizing, secular humanist groups to have their heyday. And they did. In Britain, radical laws were passed. For example, in 1965, there was the Abolition of Death Penalty Act. In 1967, the Sexual Offences Act decriminalized homosexuality. Censorship of the theatre was abolished in 1968, and in 1969, the Divorce Act liberalized divorce. All that occurred within five years. Society was changing, and it was changing fast. Abortion law reform was on the agenda too.

6.3 The Abortion Law Reform Association

But another of the seeds of the Abortion Act 1967 was sown some thirty years earlier. In 1936, just three women had formed the Abortion Law Reform Association (ALRA). For the next three decades, its membership was to remain small, at between only two and three hundred. Then in 1966, under new leadership, it flourished and grew to about 1,000 members. They were mainly well-educated women, several were medically-qualified, and about a third had already had abortions. Most had come from conventional religious backgrounds, but the majority now regarded themselves as atheists, or agnostics, or 'freethinkers'. That is, they were quite unlike the vast majority of UK women—indeed, ALRA members were a distinct elite.

Yet, this tiny, tiny group was largely responsible for the massive change in our abortion laws. How did they do it? They exerted their influence by three main means; by publishing newsletters, by educating women's groups, and by writing to the press. They were knowledgeable, they were dedicated, and they were persistent. There are lessons for all of us here.

6.4 Children as a disaster

This sinister notion gained a wider acceptance as the twentieth century rolled on. The idea was expressed that, for some children, it would have been 'better not to have been born'. This was an ideological product of the eugenics movement, fashionable from the end of the nineteenth and the beginning of the twentieth centuries. Its ethos was reinforced by the thalidomide tragedy during the early 1960s. This drug had been used as a sedative by European pregnant women in order to overcome morning sickness. But it had a teratogenic side-effect on the unborn which resulted in about 400 children in the UK, and 3,000 in Germany being born with serious deformities, like stunted, or even no, limbs. Compassion, that was popular, but in its way utterly false, decreed that for such children it would have been 'better not to have been born'.

Added to this was the growing idea that children could, quite justifiably, be unwanted, unloved, and uncared for. While much of this was myth and mischief, there was during the 1960s undoubtedly an increase in broken homes, divorce, and career ambitions among women—children were no longer necessarily the centre of traditional family life. They were becoming unwelcome. They were no longer safe. The 'new causes' of women's liberation, sexual freedom, world population, and pollution all helped to formulate and promote the idea that children could be a nuisance, a tragedy, and even a disaster.

6.5 The lever of hard cases

During the 1960s some leading medical and legal authorities, such as the Royal Medico-Psychological Association and the American Law Institute, were suggesting a little relaxing of abortion law on both sides of the Atlantic. In particular, attention was directed at the so-called hard cases, like physical and mental health, incest, rape, and genetic defect. At the same time, doctors, and especially psychiatrists, were increasingly using women's mental health as a justification for procuring abortions. What in fact was developing among this academic and medical elite was a quality of life ethic at the expense of human life itself. Although it was common knowledge that 'hard cases make bad law', they were being used as powerful levers to hasten wholesale changes of abortion laws.

6.6 The practice of illegal abortion

This was usually, but not always, the so-called 'backstreet abortion', which could lead to sterility, general ill-health, and even death. Pro-abortionists argued that legalizing abortion would clean up the backstreet. However, there was good evidence that the numbers of backstreet abortions were actually in decline even before the 1967 Act. How many of these illegal abortions actually occurred each year is still a contentious topic. Estimates for the UK vary from 10,000 to 250,000. A 1966 report from the Royal College of Obstetricians and Gynaecologists estimated 14,000. Similarly, the numbers of women who died, or who were severely injured, at the hands of criminal abortionists are contested data. Contrary to much of the propaganda from pro-abortionists, one of their chief exponents, David Paintin considered that, '... that side of abortion has to some extent been exaggerated. Most illegal abortionists in the 1960s were really quite skilful.'

Whatever the true numbers, such activities were used to scare the general public and to press home the perceived need for a revision of the abortion laws. Half-truths began to acquire the ring of truth, and although people were being largely misled, many were being disturbed.

Incidentally, the fear of a return to the so-called backstreet, with its images of old crones, coat-hangers, hot baths, and bottles of gin, is still used sometimes to abuse those who wish to limit abortion and repeal its laws. Such an argument is spurious for at least four reasons. First, for abortion to become illegal again it will have to be accompanied by a change of heart and mind among the general population—the prerequisite will be a more pro-life society, which would welcome such pro-life legislation. Second, any return to the backstreet, though criminal, would be technologically safer now. After all, there are thousands of doctors out there who are very skilled in abortion procedures, and a few 'bent' ones would keep the backstreet safe. Third, 'easy, legal abortion' created a new clientele among women who would previously never have contemplated abortion if it had remained illegal. The unthinking response of many was, 'If it's legal, it must be OK.' Fourth, there has been a recent rise in the numbers of 'chemical abortions', using relatively new and readily-available abortifacients, such as RU-486; these will lessen the demand for backstreet abortions of a surgical nature. The 'old backstreet' will never emerge again.

6.7 Inequalities in medical practice

Today, we might call this something like 'postcode medicine'. The fact was that, in the early and mid-twentieth century, some doctors performed abortions and some did not, depending largely on their personal views of medicine, law, and religion. The role of the psychiatrist was often pivotal because the only way to obtain a lawful abortion, apart from serious medical conditions, was on a psychiatrist's recommendation. The threat of a mother's suicide was an additional pressure sometimes used to cajole doctors to abort. As one doctor recalled the advice of the day was, 'Bring your daughter back when you find her with her head in the gas oven. And a suicide note would help!' Also there was seemingly one law for the rich, and another for the poor. That is, having 100 or 200 guineas and knowing the 'right' person were often the best ways to obtain an abortion. Such inequalities incensed members of the Labour Party as well as the 'free-thinkers' of ALRA, who exploited them to press for reform.

6.8 The role of contraception

In 1965, Sir Dugald Baird, the eminent gynaecologist and abortionist, coined the phrase, 'the tyranny of excessive fertility'. Women in post-war Britain tended to complete their families by the time they were twenty to twenty-five years old. So they were then faced with about eighty per cent of their fertile, married lives ahead of them, often without adequate and reliable contraception.

The most common form of contraception, the condom, had put the onus of responsibility upon the man. The introduction of the contraceptive pill, which appeared in Britain in 1961, shifted this onus to the woman. For the first time in history, not only was sexual intercourse becoming more reliably separated from procreation, but also women were moving into the sexual 'driving seat', and were beginning to control their own fertility. These were changes that were to rock society. Sex was everywhere. Sexual freedom, premarital sex, promiscuity, cohabitation, and much more were the revolutionary ingredients of this sexual upheaval. Today, by contrast, these activities are regarded merely as 'alternative lifestyle choices', but in the 1960s, they were social dynamite.

But how could you be one of the 'sexually liberated' without the encumbrance of getting pregnant? Overcoming fertility in an increasingly sexually-permissive age was the problem. The old and new contraceptive methods were the generally-accepted ways and when they failed, or were misused, or even unused, then abortion became the escape route, the backstop, for many pregnant girls and women. The 1960's bioethical equation was quite simple: more permissive sexual intercourse = more demand for abortions.

6.9 Rex v. Bourne

Many had thought of challenging the laws on abortion. One such notable person was Aleck Bourne, an obstetrical surgeon at St Mary's Hospital, London. He became the defendant in Rex v. Bourne, a most odd, but far-reaching legal case. In 1938, on 27 April, a fourteen-year-old girl, referred to as Miss H., was walking with friends outside Wellington Barracks in London. Some soldiers invited her in to see a horse with a green tail. Sadly, she was raped. She was so physically traumatized by this, that she was admitted to hospital. She was now presumed to be pregnant. Aleck Bourne kept her in St Mary's Hospital for several days, and on the eighth day, he operated.

He was arrested and what followed was an historic trial at the Old Bailey before Mr Justice Macnaghten. Bourne was charged under the Offences Against the Person Act 1861: '... whosoever, with intent to procure the miscarriage of any woman ... shall unlawfully use any instrument ... shall be guilty of felony ...'. After a two-day trial, he was acquitted. But it was a most dubious decision. Nevertheless, the case established the foundation upon which an increasing number of abortions were performed for the next thirty years.

In his celebrated summing-up, Mr Macnaghten initially questioned the meaning of a word from the Act, under which Bourne was charged, namely, 'unlawfully'. His assessment of Bourne's action was, 'A man of the highest skill, openly, in one of our great hospitals, performs the operation ... as an act of charity, without fee or reward.' The judge's inference was, could this be acting 'unlawfully', or was the defendant acting '... in good faith for the purpose only of preserving her life'? This raised Mr Macnaghten's second question. It was already established that both the 1861 and the 1929 Acts allowed a pregnancy to be terminated 'for the purpose only of preserving the life of the mother'. But Mr Macnaghten questioned the difference of meaning of the two phrases, used by counsel throughout the trial, 'danger to life' and 'danger to health' of the mother. He confessed that he could not properly understand the discussion, 'Since', he argued, 'life depends upon health'. Furthermore, he maintained, that if a doctor considered that the 'continuance of the pregnancy will ... make the woman a physical and mental wreck', then an abortion is justified 'for the purpose of preserving the life of the mother'. In other words, the phrase 'preserving the life of the mother' was interpreted by the judge to be far wider than just saving her from an imminent death; it also meant preserving her long-term physical and mental health. The case thus turned on whether or not Bourne performed the abortion 'in good faith for the purpose of preserving the [physical and mental] health of the girl.' The jury decided he did, and he was judged 'not guilty'. So, Rex v. Bourne established this as a new legal basis for the so-called 'therapeutic' abortion. As a result, the door to abortion was pushed open considerably wider.

However, there is a strange twist to the story of Aleck Bourne. He was once a member of ALRA's medico-legal committee, but later he switched sides and became a member of the executive committee of the pro-life group, the Society for the Protection of Unborn Children (SPUC). He believed that his acquittal in 1938 had had an undesirable effect and he later stated that he was, 'strongly opposed to abortion for purely social or trivial indications.'

6.10 The pro-life and medical lobbies

There was no organized pro-life counterpart to ALRA for thirty years, that is, until the 1967 Abortion Act was being debated. Then SPUC was formed. It gathered together a 0.5 million-signature petition asking Parliament to set up a Royal Commission to research the abortion issue before the law was amended. But, in reality, it was too little, too late.

The medical fraternity (and interestingly, it was men who were, and still are, in most Western societies, chiefly involved in the provision of abortion) had mixed feelings and convictions. Psychiatrists declared themselves largely in favour of termination up to twelve weeks; in hindsight, a rather mild demand. But even they were still against abortion on the grounds of inconvenience alone. Much of the medical profession was largely conservative. For example, the Royal College of Obstetricians and Gynaecologists was not keen on a law change. The British Medical Association was somewhat more liberal, but it wanted considerable conditions to be fulfilled before an abortion took place, and then only on the grounds of the health of the mother and serious abnormality of the baby. Still there was no mention of 'social considerations', which were to become the major ground for abortions, post-1967.

6.11 The 1967 Abortion Act

No British government had been keen to grasp the political nettle of abortion law reform. Instead, for several years, various private members had introduced reforming Bills, but they had all foundered. Then in 1966, David Steel MP sponsored his own private member's Medical Termination Bill.

The Bill was debated long and hard and was considerably amended during its passage through Westminster. Eventually, with Parliamentary time being given by the Labour government of the day to ensure its success, the Act was passed, and it received the Royal Assent on 27 October 1967. Six months later, on 27 April 1968, it came into operation. One year after this, its sponsor, David Steel, speaking at an ALRA meeting, said that the Bill was successful because, 'The right men were in the right place at the right time.' Counter to this, is the dismal fact that the number of evangelical Christian leaders who 'saw the issue' and stood up and spoke up against the Bill could be counted on the fingers of one hand.

The Act was, and still is, regarded by many, not only as a compromise, but also as a poorly-drafted piece of legislation. This may have suited the purposes of the pro-abortionists, because over the years most of its intended legal boundaries have been ridden over, roughshod. It has become a leaky legal bucket that now holds virtually no water of restraint. No fewer than fifteen attempts have been made to amend the Act, including the best-known private member's Bills introduced by John Corrie in 1979, and by David Alton in 1987. Basically, they proposed lowering the upper time limit for abortion to twenty and eighteen weeks, respectively. Both failed.

The 1967 Abortion Act gave no right to a woman to an abortion, and it imposed no duty on any doctor to carry out an abortion. However, it did protect a doctor from prosecution who performed an abortion, as long as two doctors certified that, in their opinion, formed in good faith, the continuation of the pregnancy involved any of the following six grounds:

1. risk to life of the woman
2. risk of injury to physical or mental health of the woman
3. risk of injury to physical or mental health of existing child(ren) greater than if the pregnancy were terminated
4. substantial risk of child being born seriously handicapped
5. in emergency—to save the life of the woman
6. in emergency—to prevent grave permanent injury to physical or mental health of the woman.

The Act also contained a 'conscience clause' to enable doctors and nurses to opt out of performing, or assisting in, abortions.

The 1967 Abortion Act was to become a ground-breaking, even shattering, piece of legislation. It is therefore instructive to re-examine four of the most popular arguments in favour of reform. During the Parliamentary debates, the abortionists said first, that easier abortion would decrease the illegitimacy rate, then at less than ten per cent. Currently this is about forty per cent, and rising. Second, they said it would lessen child battering because 'every child would be a wanted child'. Unfulfilled. Third, they said it would decrease the number of children in care, and fourth, they said it would decrease violent crime associated with sex and against children. Again, unfulfilled and unfulfilled.

While no one would argue that the Act's 'easy abortion' has been the sole cause of these disturbing social trends, it is striking that these promised benefits, from the Act's most enthusiastic devotees, have proved to be empty. Certainly, abortion nowadays is not carried out for those women that the Act's proponents professed to help and protect, namely, the overstressed, sick mother with a large family, poor housing, and little financial support. Today, abortion is mainly for young, single, childless, healthy women.

6.12 The Human Fertilisation and Embryology Act 1990
In 1984, the Warnock Report, with its liberal recommendations, was published and presented to Parliament. Bioethical battle was again enjoined at Westminster, this time to protect the human embryo. Pro-life private member's Bills in 1985, 1986, and 1987 were introduced by Enoch Powell, Ken Hargreaves, and Alistair Burt, respectively. These would have outlawed any attempts to create, store, or use human embryos other than to assist a woman to become pregnant. But they all failed.

Instead, the Human Fertilisation and Embryology Act 1990 was passed. Although this Act dealt primarily with issues of reproductive technology, human embryo experimentation, and the licensing of clinics and research facilities, its Section 37 amended the Abortion Act 1967. It altered the old grounds for abortion of 1 to 6 to the new A to G. It inserted a twenty-four-week limit for abortion on both grounds C (old ground 2) and D (old 3). It also introduced an additional ground, ground B, 'to prevent grave permanent injury to the physical or mental health of the woman.' This ground has no time limit. This 'no time limit' was also extended to grounds A (old ground 1) and E (previously ground 4), so that abortions where there is 'substantial risk of the child being born seriously handicapped', can now be performed up to birth.

The latest official figures from the Office for National Statistics (2000) show the following grounds and their associated numbers of abortions:

- (A) 95
- (B) 1,847
- (C) 168,638
- (D) 10,810
- (E) 1,859
- (F) 0
- (G) 1

Much could be, and has been, written about these shameful figures, but just three observations will be noted here. First, these data demonstrate that the vast majority (ninety-two per cent) of abortions are justified under ground C, the 'social clause'. Second, just one per cent of all abortions are performed under ground E, the 'handicap clause'. Third, these may be just figures to a statistician, but to many they represent real unborn children, who have had their lives snuffed out.

This 1990 Act also legalized the practice of selective reduction of pregnancies. Additionally, it paved the way for 'medical terminations' by abortifacients, like RU-486 (mifepristone), and it also allowed these to be administered in places other than hospitals and approved clinics.

6.13 The US situation

The American situation was somewhat different, but the same trends in thinking and practice can be detected and traced out. On 22 January 1973, some five years after our landmark Act, the Supreme Court of the United States decided in the two cases of Roe v. Wade and Doe v. Bolton. The outcome was the creation of a new liberty, the right of a woman to obtain an abortion at any time. During the first six months of a pregnancy, a woman needed *no* reason, but in the last three months she could have an abortion for *any* reason. This is abortion-on-demand, US-style, and nowadays there are about 1.5 million abortions performed each year in that country.

And there are interesting twists in this story too. In 1995, Norma McCorvey (alias Jane Roe), the pregnant woman at the centre of the historic Roe v. Wade case, reported that she had found God, left her job at an abortion clinic in Texas, and turned pro-life. She felt that she had been used as a pawn by the pro-choice movement during the court battles of the 1970s. Similarly, Sandra Cano (alias Mary Doe, of Doe v. Bolton fame) considered that she too had been 'set up' by some women attorneys who were simply looking for somebody, anybody, to further their own pro-abortion ambitions. Both women now regret their part in legalizing US abortion. Norma McCorvey has subsequently stated, 'I think abortion is wrong ... I just have to take a pro-life position.' Sandra Cano has said, 'I am against abortion. Abortion is murder.'

See, it *is* true, history can teach us something—in fact, many valuable lessons. This historical account may seem rather depressing. Indeed, the truth is that the pro-life movement in the UK has had no serious political or legal success for thirty years and more. But that is not the end. During the nineteenth century, the fight against slavery took many, many years, and much hard work by the evangelicals of the Clapham Sect and other co-belligerents, before abolition was eventually realized in 1807. Our day will come. There will be a time when the 1967 Abortion Act will be seen for what it is: a cruel, discriminatory, deadly piece of legislation. One day, people will look back and ask, 'How could a seemingly-civilized society pass such a terrible law?' In that happy day, we will marvel at all human life, and we will cherish and protect every one of our offspring. May that day come soon!

What of the future?

In the previous chapter, we looked backwards to learn some bioethical lessons from recent history. Now we look forwards to try and spot some of the future issues and trends in order to prepare us for the days to come—forewarned is forearmed, as they say.

7.1 Will it get any better?

The answer, at least in the short-term, is, no. The culture of death is now so firmly rooted in our society's thinking and practice that it cannot be uprooted overnight, or, more to the point, perhaps not even within the next decade or two. The truth is that we have seen only the blossom, there is yet considerable capacity for the culture of death to grow, and develop, and eventually to produce its full fruit.

Therefore, we must face it—currently, we are in a bioethical pit. Moreover, there is no point in mincing our words; much of the blame for this mess lies at the doorstep of the evangelical Christian church. Even that is a bit too impersonal—much of the blame lies with evangelical Christians. And if we complain and say something like, 'It's nothing to do with me', or 'It can't be my fault, I've done nothing to deserve this', then not only our inaction, but also our very words condemn us.

How different it could have been if the estimated one million and more evangelical Christians in the UK had responded with principled compassion, in biblical ways. Instead, during the last forty or more years, many evangelical Christians have been so absorbed with secondary issues like, interdenominational bickerings, and even tertiary issues like, well, you name your own trivial pursuits, that they have had little time, or energy, to tackle bioethical issues. The church and its people have been largely unaware of what was going on in the world. This has meant that now we are having to fight a rearguard action, and that is always much more difficult.

But, there is always, and it is a comforting doublet, Christian hope. Thinking and practice can change. A society's, a church's, as well as an individual's, mindset can be reformed. Remember the global influence for good caused by the New Testament church, the Reformation, and the eighteenth-century revivals? We are still feeling the positive ripples of these movements today. Who, in the eighteenth century, would have thought that the well-ingrained practice of slavery would have ended in the following century? Or who, thirty years ago, would have thought that evangelicals today would be interested in responding to bioethical issues?

So all is not lost. Although the culture of death does seem in the ascendance, that is not the whole picture. More and more people are becoming pro-life. Pro-life organizations are reporting increasing membership and activities. And the flow is entirely one way. I have still not met anyone who was once pro-life, who has now shifted to the other camp; but I know of many who have made the reverse journey. Yes, there are glimmers of hope for the future. A survey entitled, *Members' Attitudes to Abortion* was conducted by the Christian Medical Fellowship in the late 1990s. To the question, 'When does human life have full value?', about seventy per cent of the Christian student doctors answered 'at fertilization', whereas less than forty per cent of Christian practising doctors gave that answer. Furthermore, the student doctors were invariably more pro-life in their attitudes towards abortion than their older mentors. But these positive changes are occurring not just among Christians in the medical profession. Up to a third of all newly-qualified UK doctors are choosing not to perform abortions. The generation, who grew up with abortion, are beginning to reject it. The world 'belongs' to the next generation of men and women, medical and otherwise. Let us pray for them and encourage them to stand steadfast and to live by the non-negotiable truths of the Word. Yes, there is Christian hope.

And there is also Christian failure. But recognizing and acknowledging such past failure and then moving on is the proper Christian response. This is not a case of wishful thinking, or idle forgetfulness, it is an important precept of the Christian life: 'But one thing I do: Forgetting what is behind and straining towards what is ahead, I press on towards the goal to win the prize for which God has called me heavenwards in Christ Jesus' (Philippians 3:13-14). In the face of the culture of death, such a biblical strategy will keep us from discouragement, despondency, and inaction.

7.2 More of the same—bad

So, there can be little doubt that, for the foreseeable future, the thinking and the practices of the culture of death will be with us. And there will not be much change in most of its dominions.

The annual number of abortions performed in the UK will probably remain at about 180,000—indeed, this figure has changed little over the last decade. Similarly, the rate of abortions in the UK has hovered around 13.2 abortions per 1,000 women, aged between fourteen and forty-nine years old. The number of teenage pregnancies in the UK, currently more than 90,000 in total, including 8,000 girls under sixteen years old and 2,200 under fourteen, as well as their rate, about 60 per 1,000 girls, which is the highest in Western Europe, and with around thirty-five per cent of them ending in abortion, will continue to perplex governments.

Increases in sexually-transmitted diseases (STDs), 14,000 reported in England in 1990 and 20,000 in 1998, will also cause consternation at the Department of Health. These STDs are not just embarrassing, they are serious because some of them can cause infertility and life-threatening complications during pregnancy. Despite the evident failure of so much so-called sex education in schools, which in reality has been little more than the promotion of a pill and condom culture, nothing much will change on this front either. The promotion of chastity, which truly is the only effective and ethical way of limiting teenage pregnancies, will remain a concept foreign to most legislators and educators.

Chastity, marriage, and fidelity are due, long overdue, for a classroom comeback. Alongside these, we need to recapture the joys of motherhood, and fatherhood. Being pregnant is not a disease. Yet few seem to talk about the wonders and delights of fertility, motherhood, and fatherhood. We have allowed Christian teaching and Christian values to be squeezed out from our schools and to be replaced by this 'sex education', or, as it is sometimes referred to in government circles, 'teenage fertility management'. Nowadays, a woman's fertility is too often seen as a curse of nature that only contraception, backed up by abortion, can control. This is not sex education, it is *anti*-natal education. So why should not Christian ideals be taught positively in our schools, and, yes, in our churches too?

Infanticide will also continue to be a constant feature of the coming years. It will occur probably at the same rate, whatever that is. It is an unknown quantity and we know about only the tip of its iceberg because it usually occurs behind closed doors. Behind hospital doors, it is when morally-sensitive nurses are so disgusted by what they see and hear that they inform the police. Behind house doors, it is when cases, which, according to some experts could amount to over 100 a year in the UK, come before the courts.

So, not much change in the enterprises of abortion and infanticide. Yet these, and especially abortion, are also tied up with other, quite different, global problems. Population growth and demographic changes have exercised the minds of many trendspotters during the last century.

The fear of overpopulation has now taken a curious turn, in fact, a U-turn. In more and more countries of the developed world the problem has become quite the reverse—they are experiencing zero, or even negative, growth rates. This 'below replacement' growth rate is already a serious problem in countries as diverse as Italy, Latvia, and Japan. Italy, for example, faces a projected twenty-eight per cent reduction in its population over the next fifty years; the figure for the UK is four per cent. Low fertility is the principal reason for this 'new' phenomenon. Low fertility rates have many causes—economic choices and social strictures mean smaller families, career opportunities for women mean that couples are postponing starting their families until later, infertility is then often being diagnosed too late to treat, and so on. And, of course, abortion is directly reducing child numbers.

Alongside these changes in population, changes in demography have also been quietly occurring. The result is that most Western countries now have a 'top-heavy' demographic structure. This is economically and socially unhealthy. A healthy demographic pattern is like a pyramid—lots of young at the base and fewer elderly at the apex. Today, many countries have stood this pattern on its head—their demographic pattern is like an inverted pyramid. This means that the needs of a growing elderly, non-working population are having to be supplied by a decreasing, young, working population. The elderly are growing in age and in numbers— more people are getting older. In 1999, Queen Elizabeth II sent out 3,729 congratulatory birthday messages to British centenarians compared with only 255 in 1952. This increased longevity is mainly as a result of medical advances and improvements in social facilities. Substantial immigration and/or increasing the retirement age may be needed to ameliorate this problem. But, of course, abortion has also exacerbated this demographic dilemma. In the UK, for example, it has 'taken away' at least five million of our youngsters, much of the base of our pyramid is missing. This has occurred within the last thirty years—they are like 'a missing generation, within a generation'.

Infertility will also continue to be a pressing problem for many. The effects of pollution over the last decades may well emerge as a major contributing cause. But so will self-inflicted factors, like smoking, alcohol and other drug abuse, stress, sexually-transmitted diseases, previous abortions, and so on. This increased recognition of infertility, as well as society's escalating desire to 'quality control' the genetics of its posterity's embryos, will continue to drive the IVF industry. Herein lies a conflict because IVF will still be too complex and too costly a procedure. What we need to overcome the problems of most of the estimated 250,000 infertile UK couples in the age group twenty-four to thirty-five, are much simpler, low-tech methods. IVF is not, and never will be, the panacea for infertility.

7.3 More of the same—good

Several low-tech methods have already proven themselves to be effective. One form of infertility, affecting an estimated 15,000 UK couples, is known as recurrent spontaneous abortion. This is a condition whereby getting pregnant is no problem, but a miscarriage invariably occurs during mid-gestation. It is caused by a cross-immunological reaction between the father and the mother. So, a low-tech answer is for the husband to give blood and this is used to immunize his wife. Early results showed that nearly eighty per cent of women on this treatment went to term with a normal pregnancy, after as many as eight previous, consecutive miscarriages. Another example of low-tech infertility work is that of the LIFE Health Centre at Liverpool. Its treatment, based on Natural Procreative Technology (the NaPro method), assesses and then treats hormonal and organic problems underlying a couple's infertility. Though not suitable for all causes of infertility, it is recording some excellent results, better than most IVF clinics. And it incurs no human embryo abuse, it is low cost, it is non-invasive, and it is woman and child-friendly. Low-tech methods can also be important in the area of preventative medicine. For instance, dietary supplements of folic acid for women, taken both pre-conceptually and in the early days of pregnancy, have had the most dramatic effect on decreasing the incidence of neural tube defects, including spina bifida, in babies. This 'treatment' is simplicity itself, and it does avoid even the thought of abortion for many.

Another continuing good will be the caring initiatives already established by pro-life people. These include pregnancy care centres, hospices for young and old, homes for the mentally and physically disabled, and for the aged. In the near future, additional, more complex facilities, like infertility clinics and, as the culture of death spreads, health centres, and even hospitals, providing comprehensive, pro-life medical care, will be needed.

Alongside this practical caring will be the on-going work of pro-life education and agitation. There is also praying, and joining and giving. Will we be sufficient to rise to the coming challenges from the culture of death?

7.4 More of something different—bad

The big 'new' bioethical issue of the coming years will definitely be euthanasia. Before long, there will be legislative changes in the UK. Voluntary euthanasia will be legalized, perhaps in only a limited way at first, but the door will be opened wider than at present. After all, the currently-approved practice of picking off a few elderly or PVS patients, who are to be denied food and drink, or resuscitation, is a pretty powerful preview of future policy. The push for euthanasia will be helped along by living wills and advance directives being given increasing credence. These are but cruel euphemisms to make euthanasia appear decent as, in the minds of many, the 'right to die' gradually becomes the 'duty to die'. Such bits of paper, containing the patient's earlier intentions, will be easily abused, they will override a doctor's clinical judgement, they will ignore new treatments, and they will bypass what is in the current best interests of the patient. Their enforcement will be the very antithesis of good medicine. The general introduction of euthanasia will also be helped along by the UK authorities developing a bioethical blind eye to what is really happening, as has occurred in the Netherlands for many years.

Or, it may get even worse. Voluntary euthanasia will lead to non-voluntary. How long before the elderly are too frightened to go into hospital? The simple, utilitarian cure for this demographic skew and its attendant problems, outlined above, is to promote euthanasia; it matters little whether it is voluntary or non-voluntary. That would cut the numbers of the elderly. It has already been estimated that fifty per cent of lifetime medical costs typically occur in the last year or two of a person's life. Someone, somewhere in Whitehall will have done the sums. It could be presented as a double whammy—it would restore the demographic balance, and it would save huge sums of money!

The practice of medicine is about to undergo another sea change. As a result of the Human Genome Project, the flavour of medicine in the twenty-first century will be genetic medicine.

One spin-off from genetic medicine will be novel forms and uses of genetic screening. Within the next decade, all of us will probably have undergone some new forms of genetic testing. How long will it be before we are all carrying our genomic data on a microchip on a credit card in our back pocket, or handbag? Producing children will then become more technologically controlled, and much less fun. Putative parents will have their genomes checked for genetic compatibility. Embryos, conceived, of course, by IVF, will be subjected to the rigours of quality control by preimplantation genetic diagnosis (PGD). And just to make sure that the children meet all the requirements of the parents, and of society, they will be re-screened, both as unborn and born—those who do not make the genetic grade will, of course, be destroyed. If you thought that eugenics was some out-of-date practice, think again, it is here to stay for a long time yet. This will be the true coming of the age of the designer baby, and the baby as a commodity.

The closing years of the twentieth century recorded some bizarre cases of assisted reproductive techniques and parenthood. The early years of this century will do the same, but even more extreme. I challenge you to spot the future winners. How about castrating all pre-pubescent boys, freezing their gamete-producing cells, and letting them reproduce by IVF at the behest of the State? That would solve the teenage pregnancy problem. Ah, but the catch is that older men would then impregnate teenage girls. So, better still, now that we have the technology to freeze and thaw ova successfully, why not remove and freeze all ova from teenage girls and return them only if and when 'breeding' is allowed? Or what about a lesbian couple (Jean and Ovida), who, rather than using donated sperm, use reproductive cloning techniques to transfer Jean's genetic material to one of Ovida's denucleated ova? If Ovida carries the baby, who must be a girl because she is derived from Jean's genes, the child would have two biological mothers. Or, what about using cell nuclear replacement (CNR) to produce a cloned embryo from a woman, harvest the embryo's stem cells, reprogramme them to become sperm-producing cells and use the sperm to inseminate her? The mother would then also be the father—one person, both parents. Or again, what about two men having a baby, without a mother? Cloning procedures could introduce a sperm nucleus, from one man, into a donor ovum to produce a 'male egg'. This could be fertilized with sperm from the other man by IVF techniques, the embryo could be transferred to a surrogate, and bingo, a baby with two fathers? You think this is wacky? Then let me tell you that scientists have already discussed its feasibility. Or, what about having embryos implanted in men and letting them carry babies to term? Right, that's enough of that!

If, in the near future, we are going to respond effectively to the culture of death then it will be at an increasing personal cost. The world of PC, of political correctness, is becoming an enemy of the Christian. In the years to come, it will be even harder to make our bioethical stand as individuals. Not long ago, I was summoned to appear before my head of department. Apparently, an undergraduate student had written a letter complaining about my approach to teaching bioethical issues—it was allegedly biased because I had made reference to the impact of Christianity upon bioethical thinking and practice, throughout the ages. 'But how can anyone teach the history of bioethics, or, for that matter, any other subject, properly without referring to the Christian influence?', I asked. No answer was given. My lecture notes were examined and found to contain less than three per cent of what might be construed as Christian content. I was told to go and remove such bias. 'But then that *would* make my lectures biased', I complained. 'Go!', I was told. Incidentally, though I repeatedly asked to see the complaining letter from the student, it was never produced—of course not. Now we must not develop a siege mentality, or a persecution complex, but we need to be aware that for many in our post-modern world, truth is largely irrelevant. For many today, truth is not even a consensus, now it no longer exists in any objective shape or form. And for many, Christianity, with its emphasis on truth, is a foe to be suppressed. Yet, how sad that even in our universities, historically, the last bastions of free-speech, the PC thought-police are beginning to run the show. Beware; the honest and upright will be persecuted. In the coming years, good men and women will be at a premium.

7.5 More of something different—good
Genetic medicine is not all gloom and doom—it will also bring about striking benefits. Currently, doctors generally treat the *effects* rather than the *causes* of a particular disease. Genetic medicine will allow doctors, for the first time, to begin to understand the cause and the development, or the pathogenesis, of diseases. Perhaps within the next decade, most of the genetic factors involved in common human diseases will be defined and this information will be used to clarify the biological mechanisms involved, and hasten new treatments. Pharmaceutical and biotechnology industries will be able to use this information to design better-targeted drugs. This will alter everyday medicine as we currently know it. But, a word of caution, medical and scientific researchers have consistently displayed a nasty habit of promising more than they can ever deliver. For instance, the promises of the relatively-simple procedure of xenotransplantation, using genetically-modified organs, like pig's hearts, for humans, have, after decades of intense research and optimism, yet to be fulfilled. Other technical problems, currently unknown, will also surface and cause delay in achieving some of these much-vaunted advances in genetic medicine; but they will come, and we may all benefit.

Another string in the bow of genetic medicine is gene therapy and this will be at the leading edge of attempting to cure dozens of diseases. But today's gene therapy procedures are too specialized, too labour-intensive, and too expensive. Gene therapy will only have a major impact when vectors to carry the altered genes are developed that can, for example, be safely injected into patients, like some diabetics use insulin now. An ever-growing range of diseases will undoubtedly be treatable, but it will be for the thousands of patients, rather than for the millions. We should also remember that as radical as gene therapy is, it cannot cure *all* human diseases, world-wide—most are caused by other agents, such as micro-organisms and malnutrition.

You and I cannot escape being part of this 'More of something different—good'. We must not run away with the idea that things will only get worse—that is unbiblical defeatism, non-Christian pessimism (1 John 5:4-5). Nor must we resign ourselves to the idea that because everything is in God's hands, we need do nothing—that is so-called hyper-Calvinism, which leads to a sterile indifference (Matthew 22:29). Nor must we think that our efforts alone will be sufficient—that is mere humanism, which ignores the scope of our struggle (Ephesians 6:12-13). Such views betray faulty theology. We need to wrestle with the antimony of the sovereignty of God *and* the responsibility of man, and act upon them. The future bioethical landscape depends upon God *and* upon us. If we do nothing, it certainly will be a poor show. On the other hand, ...! So, what will *you* be doing, during the next ten years, to bring about something different, something good, something in the culture of life?

Well, this has been but a glimpse at a few of the up-and-coming bioethical issues. Nobody can foresee the future, and neither you nor I can predict all the approaching trends and swerves. Nevertheless, we know that the immediate future does look bleak. The culture of death has taken root—the notion that some human beings are sub-standard, subhuman, and worthless is now believed by many. But I continue to expect that the final outcome will be quite different. Truth will eventually out. Principled compassion will win the day. Another generation will be grateful that we stood firm. There will be a better bioethical day. And it will come even sooner if we all learn to respond to the culture of death, in a Christlike manner.

So what can we do?

'When the foundations are being destroyed, what can the righteous do?'
PSALM II:3.

Over the years I have read many, and reviewed several, Christian books on bioethical issues. Almost without exception, they have had one signal weakness. Though they have usually described the issues adequately, and often expounded the Scriptures properly, they have largely ignored the next step, namely, provide answers to the question, So what can we do? That is not going to be a deficiency of this book. Here is the denouement of this primer. There are at least five responses to this question.

8.1 We must pray

'The prayer of a righteous man is powerful and effective' (James 5:16). This is Christian life-support: God does hear his people pray, and he can, and does, sovereignly change both people and situations. So prayer must be the starting-point for real change. Therefore these bioethical issues ought to be a regular part of our prayer lives, both personal and corporate.

We start with ourselves. We must pray for our own hearts, that they might be biblically-motivated, and for our own minds, that they might be biblically-informed. We must pray for those personally caught up and trapped in the awfulness of the culture of death—the pregnant, the disabled, the senile, the infertile, and so on. We must pray for those in the forefront of the battles—for doctors, hospital administrators, and especially for nurses. We must pray for believers engaged in those particular occupations that they would resist the culture of death and stand up for the culture of life. We must also pray for our leaders and decision-makers (1 Timothy 2:1-3). So, we must pray for the government, and the opposition, for the police, trade union leaders, parents, schoolteachers, employers, magistrates, '... for kings and all those in authority.' The list is almost endless.

8.2 We must educate

And the education process begins with us too. Twenty years ago, there was virtually no good Christian material available on these issues. Just about the only book on abortion was RFR Gardner's, *Abortion: The Personal Dilemma* (Paternoster Press, 1972). It was an influential, but a confused and confusing volume partly because, under certain circumstances, such as handicap, it advocated (p. 200) '... doing all we can to prevent the birth of deformed children ...', and for 'the half-caste child', it considered (p. 192) abortion as '... the wisest management for the sake of the foetus'. Nowadays, there are many first-rate, thoroughly pro-life leaflets, magazines, booklets, books, videos, and websites—see the list of Resources in chapter 10. Now there are no excuses for not getting to grips with these bioethical topics.

We need to learn some facts. For example, did you reckon that there were as many as 600 abortions every working day in England and Wales? Were you aware that thousands and thousands of human embryos are being deliberately destroyed each year? And we need to root out some myths. Abortion is not 'progressive and enlightened', as it is so often portrayed. Eugenics is not something that disappeared with the Nazis in the 1940s. Euthanasia must never be regarded as proper medical treatment.

We may need to change our attitude towards the physically and mentally disabled, the unborn, the elderly, human embryos—all those made in the image of God.

After educating ourselves, we need to educate our families; parents, brothers, sisters, grandparents, aunts, uncles, and cousins. And especially, we must educate our children. If we are parents, then in the economy of God, we are responsible for instructing our children in truth and right-eousness. And, if we ignore our responsibilities here our children will certainly pick up myths and anti-Christian ideas in the playground, classroom, and elsewhere.

If we are parents, we can also check on our schools' sex education curricula. Did you know, for example, that abortion is now a topic within the syllabuses of GCSE religious education, as well as personal and social education (PSE)? How is this taught? Is abortion being implicitly recommended to our children? What about euthanasia, surrogacy, genetic engineering, and all the other bioethical issues? Without doubt, some of these are being discussed in the classroom. It would be grievous if our children first heard about such topics from a confused teacher, rather than from you.

There are now new opportunities to become school governors, who can influence the ethical ethos of a school—if you volunteer, you will almost certainly be accepted!

We can help educate our neighbours by talking about these issues—now and again the opportunities arise, perhaps while waiting at the school gate, or at the bus stop, or in the supermarket car park. Something a little more formal would be to invite a few friends to your home for coffee and cakes and show one of the many good, short videos available from the various pro-life organizations—they can be effective conversation starters. And sometimes you will be surprised, and usually pleasantly so, by the reactions of friends and others to these life-and-death issues.

We need to educate our churches. Evangelical Christians have been slow off the mark. Where were the evangelical voices in 1967 when the Abortion Act was going through Parliament? It is only in the last twenty years that evangelicals have started to understand these issues and have been prepared to stand up and be counted. Too many have pleaded neutrality, which has perjured the truth. And churches must never be so small-minded to make the unmarried, pregnant girl so fearful of scandal that she seeks an abortion. Thankfully, this occurs less and less nowadays, but it does still happen.

Ministers and church leaders have a key role and responsibility here—we must not continue to fail our young people, and the rest of our congregations, by ignoring to teach them the Bible's foundations and responses to these issues. Too many are still confused about the bioethics of, for example, abortion or IVF treatments, and too few congregations have developed a theology of living *and* of dying.

Some churches have organized, either alone, or, better still, with other churches in their area, successful day or half-day conferences, or simple evening meetings on various bioethical issues. What about planning one for your church, your locality? There are well-informed, first-rate speakers who would be happy to be invited. Such gatherings, as well as being excellent educational exercises, can also be happy times of fellowship with others of like mind. The outcomes of such ventures can be better-educated Christians and the formulation of local strategies for future pro-life collaborative efforts.

We need to remember that Christians are not immune to abortion, infertility, and so on. Some of the estimated one-in-ten UK women, who have had abortions, and the one-in-six couples, who are infertile, as well as the parents and relatives of the handicapped will be in our congregations. And, of course, none of us is exempt from old age—we are the next, or the next but one, generation of the elderly.

We need to watch the media. We need to understand the times. We must not be naive. The British Pregnancy Advisory Service (BPAS) may sound like an admirable organization, but it is the largest supplier of abortion in the UK. What about Progress? It is a public relations operation, sponsored by pharmaceutical giants, which promotes genetic manipulation and destructive research on human embryos. And we need to learn to judge bias. We may think that in the UK we have fair and balanced media. Wrong. They are usually anti-Christian and pro-choice in their personnel, outlook, and output. Even those seemingly wholesome women's magazines, like *Woman* and *Woman's Own*, are often similar in their editorial stance and feature articles to the more outrageous pro-choice ones, such as *Cosmopolitan* and *Options*—I know because, from time to time, I stand in one of a famous chain of newsagent's shops and flick through them!

When it comes to education, we, as Christians, can be terribly lazy—we can be not only untaught, but also unteachable, students. We have this strange tendency to think that we can somehow absorb knowledge passively, a bit like sunbathing. The number and weight of books on our shelves, however theologically-sound or seminally-topical they might be, are not measures of our understanding—we actually need to open them and read them, studiously. Just consider the enthusiast; he reads, he talks, he spends time and his money on his hobby—he is actively taken up by it. So why do we fool ourselves that we will attain any decent understanding of these bioethical issues by doing very little? Remember the 1997 Labour government's three priorities for the nation: education, education, education!

8.3 We must be salt and light

The Lord Jesus Christ declared that his people are salt and light (Matthew 5:13-16). Note the two key words, 'you are'; verses 13 and 14 do not say 'you will be' or 'some might be'. *All* Christians *are* salt and light. But the ever-realistic Lord Jesus Christ warned that we can become pretty insipid, as well as rather dull. So how salty are you? Salt has that wonderful ability to stop the putrefaction and so preserve what is good. But first it has to get out of the salt cellar—it needs to be sprinkled, or even better, rubbed in. There is no room here for Christian isolationism. To stop the rot, to sting evil, Christians need to be rubbed into society. Furthermore, is your little light shining brightly? Light chases away darkness and ignorance, and it enables those people around us to see reality and truth more clearly.

As salt and light, we are called to struggle for Christian values. And you know what happens when we stop struggling? Not nothing. Non-Christian values win the day. And that is precisely where we are today in so many areas of society, particularly in terms of the culture of death. Of course, we bemoan it. Christians have too often become moaners, *par excellence*. But are we prepared to labour to bring about the necessary changes that we long for? Are we willing to work for both regeneration and reformation?

The political arena is a foreign place for most Christians. Yet, we have the franchise and, as good citizens, we should use it, carefully. The early Church had little, if any, political power and therefore never really had to face the question of what to do with it—it is quite different for us. Of course, we should not give our vote automatically to the pro-life candidate; he may be dreadful in other areas of civic and political life. But, at least, we should raise some of the great bioethical issues with him as he speaks at the hustings, or stands canvassing on our doorstep. I well remember a Parliamentary candidate and his wife having a good old intra-marital ding-dong about human embryo experimentation when I raised the topic at my front door; it was obvious they had never discussed it before, but they went away somewhat more enlightened.

We can write to, and meet with, our MPs, or AMs, or MSPs, or MLAs, or whoever. Have you ever met yours? Resolve to do so before you die, or better still, in the next year or two—it can be quite an eye-opener! If you are somewhat hesitant, then two or three of you could go together as a little delegation. All such representatives hold regular 'surgeries' and your local library and newspapers will have the details of dates, times, and places. He, or she, cannot be an expert on all subjects and many will actually welcome some reasoned input. You can at least disabuse them of the idea that to be bioethically concerned and pro-life is to be cranky! After all, who else will speak up for the unborn, the disabled, the weak, and the senile?

When writing, or speaking, to those in authority there are some basic lessons to learn. Remember, the key is communication. If you want to avoid the dreary, standard, photocopied answer, then make sure you ask a particular question, perhaps requesting some local information, or some precise, future voting intentions. And there is little point in starting a letter, as I recently saw one written to an MP: 'Do you not know what the Bible says in Genesis 1:27 ...?' The MP probably did not know, and was unlikely to be persuaded to care much either. Such ripsnorting letters will almost certainly end up in his little, round, filing cabinet, in the corner of his House of Commons' office. Such 'hot' letters may salve the consciences of some Christians, but they communicate little, and they advance the cause of Christ, and the culture of life, even less. Instead, we should be courteous and gentle, yet straightforward and winsome—no trickery, no threats. We are not point-scoring, rather we are trying to persuade a man, or a woman, that the Bible's teaching on a certain issue, and the ensuing Christian response, are both entirely reasonable and eminently workable, and that if followed the outcome would be for the betterment of all.

Of course, it may be that your MP is pro-life, and even a Christian. If so, then make the most of it and support and encourage them in their stand. And do not forget that letters of appreciation and cheerful support are a pleasure to write, and presumably to receive. We are not only men and women with grievances—Christians can be a jolly lot too—and those who have stood up and supported our bioethical stance, sometimes at considerable personal cost to themselves, deserve our admiration and our thanks, whatever their politics, religion, or failings.

Our Christian proclamation always needs to be set alongside an appeal to the hearts and minds of those in our secular society. We are living in the twenty-first century and most Parliamentarians, together with the vast majority of the population, have virtually no Christian knowledge or understanding—we must remember this. Christians have an onerous task here. The truth and the dignity of those made in the image of God are at stake. We are dealing here with the specialness of the human race. And, as Bible-believing Christians, we have been entrusted with both the diagnosis and the cure. Yet the wonder, and the comfort, is that the Christian does possess robust answers to difficult questions. We do, or at least, we should have, a proper understanding of bioethical issues. There is so much confusion within our society, but if we believe that God has a better way for human beings to live, and to die, then we must present our arguments as attractively and as cogently as possible. We need not fear men (or women).

We can check on the activities of the National Health Service and our regional and local health authorities. How do you know that another abortion clinic is not planned for your area, or even next to your church? Do you know if your local hospital performs IVF treatments? Does it have a policy on resuscitation of the elderly and infirm, or on euthanasia? Does your nearby university experiment with human embryos? We are not calling for Christians to become a band of snoopers and whistle-blowers, but we all have an obligation to exercise responsible citizenship.

From time to time, the government, or its agencies, like the Human Fertilisation and Embryology Authority (HFEA), asks for comment on particular bioethical practices, such as pre-implantation genetic diagnosis, or human cloning. Responding to these consultation papers can be an invaluable exercise, not only in clarifying our own thinking, but also because the views of those from the culture of life need to be conveyed to those in authority.

If you are a trade union member, do you know your union's policies on these bioethical issues? They may be deliberately ambiguous and non-committal, but they may not be. Check them out.

We can write letters to local and national newspapers. Letters' pages are some of the most read parts of newspapers. We can meet with the editor of our local newspaper, give her some literature and tell her about pro-life action in our area—a short write-up, accompanied by a good photograph, will usually be gratefully received. We can also contact national and local radio and television stations. Local stations often welcome pro-life comment on news' stories and once you have proved yourself, they will contact you again (and again). Of course, such activities are not for everyone, but a few of you could become real media stars. The authentic Christian voice is so rarely heard in the media these days—do not complain about it, change it!

Now, contrary to all that has gone before, some words of restraint. Strange to say, it is possible to overdo this agitation. Some pro-life people, who have become so frustrated with seeking to change, for example, abortion policy by democratic means, now consider that civil disobedience is the way forward. A few, in the USA, have even murdered doctors connected with the abortion industry—such behaviour is to be utterly abhorred and requires no further comment.

But what is to be our proper relationship to government and law with regard to these issues? Romans 13:1-7 and 1 Peter 2:13-17 are among the decisive passages of Scripture from which three principles can be drawn. First, God has commanded us to obey the State. Second, God has not set up authority and law in the State that is separate from himself. Both civil government and its law stand under the law and judgement of God. Third, the State is the agent of justice, to restrain evil and the evil-doer.

Are we then to obey the State no matter what? No! (Matthew 22:21). The bottom line is that at a certain point there is a Christian duty to disobey the State, as, for example, the early Christians did when the State of Rome insisted that they worship Caesar. But civil governments and their laws are to be resisted only when first, they command something forbidden by God, like idol-worship, and second, when they forbid something commanded by God, like preaching, or praying. Thus, the Bible commands civil law-breaking when the State requires us to sin. But the State has not required, or commanded us to kill the unborn. Do we then have a mandate to act against say, abortion clinic staff? No, our duty is to encourage, not force, others to do what is morally right. So, can we break into and disrupt an abortion clinic? No. The violation of a proper law, such as that of trespass, as a means of protesting against a rotten law, such as allowing abortion, is unworthy of Christian behaviour. It is the logic of terrorism. But does not, for example, the mass killing of the unborn demand exceptional tactics? Cannot we simply enter abortion clinics and rescue those being led away to slaughter, based on Proverbs 24:11? No. This passage of Scripture outlines an awesome responsibility, not a method. The legitimate methods before us are legion: we can pray, discuss, counsel, debate, entreat, leaflet, visit, broadcast, educate, and write. They are enough—we have not done even these yet.

Finally, we need to decide on this issue of co-belligerency, co-labouring. This frightens some Christians. Out there are many, many people who agree with us that, for example, abortion and euthanasia are wrong. They are the morally-sensitive, and many of them are the nicest folk you will ever meet. There is no compromise in working as co-belligerents with them. I have worked in the LIFE organization, with its mix of religious people, atheists, and agnostics, for twenty years and never have I had to compromise my allegiance to Christ. We are fighting the same bioethical campaign. Of course, we may come to it from quite different worldviews. Ecclesiastically, we are perhaps miles apart. We may never agree on the primary doctrines of Christianity. But, I tell you, apart from some of these people, the pro-life flame would have been snuffed out in Britain long ago. We, as rather sluggish, disengaged evangelicals, need to come to these issues with a certain amount of shame and humility—we should have been in the vanguard, but instead we have been a reluctant rearguard. And anyway, working as co-belligerents can be a most refreshing opportunity to get out of our evangelical ghettos, and meet some real unbelievers!

Come on now, you can see there is no room for apathy. There is plenty to do. You can agitate. You can be daring. You can bring salt and light to these bioethical problems. You can act creatively, thoughtfully, and effectively. Then you really will make a difference.

8.4 We must care

The watching world has many inconsistencies and deficiencies, but it is not always stupid. And it will readily tell us that there is no credibility to anything we say, or do, or object to, unless we are prepared to care.

We can care for people with problem pregnancies, disabled children, the elderly, the infirm, the senile, the infertile, whoever. The golden rule (Matthew 7:12), 'In everything, do to others what you would have them do to you' was spoken from the very lips of the Lord Jesus Christ. It was deemed such an important teaching that it was paraphrased to appear in both the Old and the New Testaments, in Leviticus 19:18 and in Matthew 22:39, as 'Love your neighbour as yourself.' This according to Paul, in Romans 13:9, is the summation of the law.

You cannot read the Scriptures without being struck by the number of times we are pressed to care, to 'do good'. Evangelical Christians have often been guilty of turning a blind eye to, or at least, demoting such injunctions. Historically, we have majored on personal salvation by faith alone and dismissed 'works' as having no part in that salvation. And, theologically, quite right too. But, to our discredit, we have gone too far, and minored on the place of 'good works' in our sanctification, which is where they belong, and centrally so.

A few passages of Scripture can help redress the balance in our thinking. For example, Titus 2:14 states that the Lord Jesus Christ wants, '... a people that are his very own, eager to do what is good.' Paul, when he bade farewell to the Ephesian elders, reminded them of his labours, 'In everything I did, I showed you that by this kind of hard work we must help the weak, remembering the words the Lord Jesus himself said: "It is more blessed to give than to receive"' (Acts 20:35). Or what about Ephesians 2:10? 'For we are God's workmanship, created in Christ Jesus to do good works, which God prepared in advance for us to do.' And Philippians 2:4 reminds us that, 'Each of you should look not only to your own interests, but also to the interests of others.'

Therefore, we are to be 'full of good works'. It is simply wrong-headed spirituality to think that the Christian life consists of nothing but witnessing and evangelism and that it is for others, the less competent, somewhere in the background, to do the caring thing. A look at the life of Christ will show us how false a notion that is. As someone has said, 'The church is the only society on earth that exists for the benefit of non-members.'

Let me give a concrete and very telling example of what I mean. In the UK, an examination of data from the Office for National Statistics shows that the average patient undergoing an abortion is a twenty-two-year-old, single woman. She goes to a non-NHS hospital, that is, a private clinic, with a nine to twelve-week-old unborn child and has an abortion by means of vacuum aspiration, under statutory ground C, the so-called 'social clause', that is, because of 'risk of injury to physical or mental health of the woman'.

But when you look at the actual medical conditions that produce the risk to her 'physical or mental health' you do not see much multiple sclerosis of the mother, pelvic deformation, diabetes, haemorrhaging, chromosomal abnormality, or rubella contact. In truth, some ninety per cent of all abortions are done for neurotic and depressive disorders, under the 'social clause'. No doubt, some of these are women who need expert medical care. But, but, but I suggest, no, I know, that the majority want, crave, and need friendship, support, love, and just someone to talk to. These are not women who are manic-depressives, or neurotics. These are women who need some love and practical care. And many, many readers could give that, couldn't you? Yes, you could!

Or, how about doing some shopping, or baby-sitting for the mother of five, with number six on the way? Or, how about visiting, reading, and talking with some elderly man, or woman? Or, how about helping the parents of a handicapped child or adult? Or, what about befriending the weak and the vulnerable? Such simple 'good works' are the fruit of recognizing their inherent preciousness, because they are made in the image of God.

Whenever we care for others with problems and difficulties, we do so as those who have ourselves failed. There is no bioethical high ground for us here. It is not our native wit or cleverness that has rescued and delivered us from the culture of death. It is God's grace. Yet there is too often a gaping chasm between our Christian declaration and our Christian doing. We may know what is the right response, but have we done it, at least, seventy times seven? It is salutary to remember that some of the Lord Jesus Christ's harshest words were against unfruitfulness, or Christian indolence— check out the parable of the talents (Matthew 25:14-30), and especially the fate of the one-talent man.

So the call is loud and clear—we must care. Already Christians are responding. There are growing numbers of believers taking on leadership roles in pro-life organizations, at both the national and local level, as chairmen, treasurers, secretaries, counsellors, and general helpers. The call, and the need, is not for detached clichés and lukewarm sympathy, but rather for rugged, straightforward, and practical Christian orthodoxy, which is best described as 'principled compassion'—the new PC.

8.5 We must join and give

There are pro-life groups almost everywhere. And if there is not one near you, then you know what to do—start one! Remember, once upon a time, every such group began with just one or two founding members. Somebody had to make the first move.

We can give of ourselves, our time, our money, and our energy. But we are not to rub sore the consciences of other men and women. I know that some are already too hard-pressed, but I also know that if many of us could cut out just, say, one hour of television per week, then we could write that letter, make that visit, or telephone that person. Similarly, many are not financially rich. Nevertheless, it is every charity's experience that it is the poor who are so often the most generous. We are all gifted—there is not one of us who cannot do something to advance the culture of life. And such involvement can be so refreshing and life-enhancing. There are latent talents to be discovered—you may be surprised how good you can be at producing a poster, organizing a coffee morning, or stuffing 200 envelopes.

Women are especially good at being directly involved, for example, in counselling at pregnancy care centres, or visiting the elderly. Men can decorate old people's homes, plan pro-life activities, and fetch and carry for fund-raising events. And what surprises there are to be had at the latter—the suit I usually wear on Sundays was a £5 bargain! Every organization needs extra people for typing, phoning, counting, driving, reading, speaking, cleaning, opening and shutting, selling and buying, serving and clearing, and so forth. And we need not fear about committing ourselves for a lifetime—why not help, for say, just a year or two? Our circumstances may change, our prospects may alter, but there are always some good works to be done somewhere, and our joining and giving can become part of our Christian service.

We really must join the struggle. We can do little on our own. Over the years, some individuals and some churches have tried. But they have generally failed, mainly because they lack the expertise, good literature, proper advice, and so on, that established organizations have already developed over many years—so why try to re-invent the wheel?

These five answers to the question, So what can we do?, are bound up in Christian duty. This is often described in Scripture as a two-part undertaking. A splendid example is found in Colossians 3, where we are told to first, put off sin and second, to put on righteousness. Its application to the realm of bioethics is clear; we are to shun the culture of death, and we are to embrace the culture of life. That is, we are to develop an ethic of avoidance *and* an ethic of engagement. Working out these answers to this big question, So what can we do?, will help us to perform our Christian duty much better.

Our response should result in little communities of people, who still maintain the dignity and sanctity of all human life, whether pre-born, born, or approaching its natural end. We should be those people, who cherish the young, and the old, and who respect the big, and the small. May God give us all the wisdom and energy to do so. May we be '... as shrewd as snakes and as innocent as doves' (Matthew 10:16).

A final word

9.1 Three groups of readers

This primer has been a call to a Christian understanding and a Christian response concerning bioethical issues. It is anticipated that there will be three groups of readers. One group will welcome it, and hopefully find it challenging, instructive, and generally useful. This group will consist largely of evangelical Christians, plus others who live under the banner of Christian, as well as the morally-sensitive—not that I flatter myself that they will all read it, as if! But I do hope that some of the latter will be convinced by this primer because its statements and arguments, though essentially Christian, should appeal to all men and women of goodwill. And these statements and arguments should appeal, primarily, because they are true.

But the second and third groups of readers will dismiss this book. The second group is numerically the largest—I shall call them 'secular humanists with a Christian memory'. They are typified by our most influential bioethicist, or moral philosopher of the last century, Baroness Warnock. Not only was she responsible for the Warnock Report, but she has written several books on ethics and bioethics, and she is regularly wheeled out by the media to comment whenever a novel story, such as a case of bizarre surrogacy, or posthumous fatherhood, breaks—as she wrote to me recently, 'I seem to spend so much time making more or less half-baked pronouncements of this kind that I lose track.' The resistance to this book by the third group of readers is much more disappointing, even to the point of distress, because they are evangelical Christians. Yet they will dismiss this book as espousing a soft 'social gospel', not something for full-blooded, Bible-believing, evangelical Christians, like them. Both groups are wrong. And I shall explain why.

9.2 *An Intelligent Person's Guide to Ethics*

This is the title of one of Mary Warnock's best-sellers. In it, she continually eschews the doctrines and practices of historic and experiential Christianity. Nevertheless, this creates a huge, insoluble problem for her because, though she is essentially a 'secular humanist', she still has 'a Christian memory'. For example, she is persuaded (p. 107), though not, it must be said, directly from the book of Genesis, that human beings are significantly different from other animals, and (p. 68) that therefore '... humans have moral priority over other animals.' She thereby rejects 'speciesism', which maintains that human beings are no different morally from other species, as '... an irrational prejudice ...' And when discussing human rights and the relationship of man to nature, she has (p. 69) high regard for the concept of '... stewardship, deriving from a long Judaeo-Christian tradition ...' She also recognizes (p. 108), though again, not as a result of the Bible's diagnosis, that our '... life is precarious, difficult and far from perfect.' She also has problems with 'rights-talk', and states (p. 74) that, '... a civil society could not function if it subsisted only on indignation where rights had been infringed ...' What we need, she concludes, is '... sympathy, kindness and generosity.' She has obviously, once upon a time, read passages from the Bible, like the Sermon on the Mount (Matthew 5-7) and she even has a distant memory of the nature of the fruit of the Spirit (Galatians 5:22-23).

Moreover, she argues (p. 69) that, '... a moral concept is best expressed in religious language ...' She admires the work of philosophers like, Aristotle, Hume, and Kant, and she concurs with the latter (p. 80), that we are dictated to by '... a relentless Protestant conscience, internal to each one of us'. Moreover, she affirms (p. 79) that in this world there are, of course, both 'good men' and 'bad men'. But, here comes her huge, insoluble problem. She is at a total loss to explain how a woman can escape the culture of death and gain the culture of life, or how a bad man can be transformed into a good one. To be ethically good, according to the Baroness (p. 87): '... requires an effort of imagination and of sympathy'. Therefore a good man will say (p. 87), '... he must act for the good of another, against his inclination and in obedience to the dictates of a "stern duty".'

How sad all this is. Her analysis of the human condition is almost correct, but only partly-formed. She is a 'secular humanist with a Christian memory'. For example, she acknowledges (p. 108) that there are

'... intrinsic flaws in the world, including flaws in [ourselves].' She also knows that we are '... subject to temptation ... the narrow goals of self-interest ...' yet we '... adopt ideals towards which we can strive.' (p. 108). This is synonymous with the Christian diagnosis, or, at least, with part of it. It is like a person struggling under conviction of sin (Romans 7:1-25). She is groping in the dark. Her bioethical system is inadequate, it is arbitrary, it is built on shifting sand, it has no firm foundation. This is the great failure of the secular humanist's worldview. She cannot, or will not, understand the immutable strength of the Bible's diagnosis plus cure. She cannot 'see' the need for Christian rebirth, Christian love, and Christian duty. She cannot grasp the need for Christ. 'What a wretched [wo]man I am! Who will rescue me from this body of death? Thanks be to God—through Jesus Christ our Lord! (Romans 7:24-25).

Such is the plight of the 'secular humanist with a Christian memory'. They can recognize the existence of many of the bioethical tangles thrown up by society, but they have no certain foundation by which to judge and respond in a consistent, and what is sometimes a costly, manner to these issues. Almost by definition, they are living in the culture of death. They will not welcome the analyses and the remedies presented in this book. They will put it down for being too narrow-minded and too artless. They will rail against its absolutes.

9.3 The full-orbed Christian

To the third group belong those Christians who consider themselves to be beyond the remit of this book. They tend to be the somewhat super-spiritual, stand-offish, cliquish people. Their main interests and activities consist of gathering together, self-examination, singing, evangelism, revival, and so on. All of these pursuits are thoroughly biblical, and I do not want to be overly harsh, but there is more to the Christian life than these somewhat introverted and isolating activities. They have not grasped the Bible's emphases on good works, and citizenship, and duty, and engagement with the world as salt and light. In truth, they are lop-sided and immature Christians. Some of my acquaintances are among this group; I know them well.

They too are wrong. There should be no conflict between witnessing for

Christ and caring for the elderly. Why cannot we attend a Bible rally one day, and discuss euthanasia with our MP the next? Christians should be in the vanguard of the much-needed regeneration and reformation of our society. Christians, who simply complain about the state of our nation, will never make any difference to it, and they will not be listened to for long, either by Christians, or by non-Christians.

Yet, there is no other group of people on this earth who should see and understand these bioethical issues in such clear focus as Bible-believing Christians. They, above all others, should understand the meaning and value of human life, from conception to natural death, and even beyond. And it is to these people that the full-orbed gospel has been entrusted— regeneration and reformation are Christian words, they are our biblical heritage. We should be praying for both, and working for both.

We need to defend the inerrancy and infallible authority of the Bible, but we also need to defend the unborn and the elderly. We need to stand up for Christ, and we need to stand up for the disabled. To compartmentalize our lives into the spiritual (such as, evangelism) and the temporal (such as, doing good) is to misunderstand the message of the Book. It is both a denial of Christ as Saviour, and a failure to accept Christ as Lord over every aspect of our lives.

Can you see what I am driving at? There are two extremes of people who will never respond properly to the culture of death. The false view of one group is to ignore the real driving force of a proper response, that is, the truths of the Bible as well as the regenerating, energizing, reforming influences of the Christian gospel. This is the state of the 'secular humanist with a Christian memory'. And the other group's false view is to misunderstand the Bible's teaching on Christian sanctification, compassion, and works. This is the state of the 'falsely spiritual', or partly-orbed Christian.

Our chief end is to glorify God and to enjoy him forever. Our chief end is to be complete, full-orbed Christians. Our chief end is to be hearers and doers of the Word. Our chief end is to *be* like him, and to *do* like him.

9.4 And, at last

And now a final, final word. When you have read this book, studied the

Bible, and some additional resources, talked over a few of the issues, and you are beginning to feel sufficiently stout-hearted, well done! You are probably pretty bioethically fit. Now get out there, and respond to the culture of death.

'This day I call heaven and earth as witnesses against you that I have set before you life and death, blessings and curses. Now choose life, so that you and your children may live and that you may love the Lord your God, listen to his voice, and hold fast to him.'

DEUTERONOMY 30:19-20.

Resources

The following resources are but a tiny fraction of those available. Nevertheless, they are some of the best and certainly they are sufficient to get you stuck into some further study of bioethical issues. Happy hunting!

10.1 Books

Burleigh, Michael (1994). *Death and Deliverance—'Euthanasia' in Germany 1900-1945*. Cambridge University Press, Cambridge.

Cameron, Nigel de S and Pamela F Sims (1986). *Abortion: the Crisis in Morals and Medicine*. Inter-Varsity Press, Leicester.

Keown, John (1997). *Euthanasia Examined: Ethical, Clinical and Legal Perspectives*. Cambridge University Press, Cambridge.

McCullagh, Peter J (1987). *The Foetus as Transplant Donor—Scientific, Social and Ethical Perspectives*. John Wiley & Sons, Chichester.

Morgan, Derek and Robert G Lee (1991). *Blackstone's Guide to the Human Fertilisation & Embryology Act 1990—Abortion & Embryo Research, The New Law*. Blackstone Press Ltd., London.

Nilsson, Lennart (1980). *A Child Is Born—Photographs of Life Before Birth: A Practical Guide for Expectant Mothers*. Faber & Faber, London.

Schaeffer, Francis A and C Everett Koop (1980). *Whatever Happened to the Human Race?* British edition. Marshall, Morgan & Scott, London. (1983) Revised US edition. Crossway Books, Wheaton, Illinois.

Warnock, Mary (1998). *An Intelligent Person's Guide to Ethics*. Duckworth, London.

10.2 Parliamentary and HMSO publications

Offences Against the Person Act 1861. Statutes Vol 25, Chapter 100, pp. 229-238.
Infant Life (Preservation) Act 1929. Statutes Vol 19, Chapter 34, pp. 773-774.
Abortion Act 1967. Statutes Vol. 2, Chapter 87, pp. 2033-2036.
Rex v. Bourne 1939. 1 King's Bench, pp. 687-696.
UK Committee of Inquiry into Human Fertilisation and Embryology (1984). (The Warnock Committee Report). HMSO, London. Cmnd. 9314.
Human Fertilisation and Embryology Act 1990. Statutes Chapter 37, pp. 1471-1509.
Human Fertilisation and Embryology Authority (HFEA) Annual Reports.
Office for National Statistics (ONS) Monitors.

10.3 Journals and magazines

Nature, *New Scientist,* and *Science* (all weekly) and *Scientific American* (monthly) are kept in the current publications section in most libraries. These are probably the best sources of news and views from a scientific viewpoint. Daily newspapers and other journals (from *Woman's Own* to *Time* magazine) can also be useful.

10.4 World-wide web sites

This is a source of millions of articles and comments, but it must be said that the vast majority are pretty poor and unsuitable. However, there are some excellent websites, like that of the *British Medical Journal* (**www.bmj.com**), which is fully searchable. Other useful sites (beware, they are not all from the culture of life), which cover bioethical issues are:

American Medical Association, **www.ama-assn.org/**
—the official site for US medical thinking and practice.

Center for Bioethics and Human Dignity, **www.bioethix.org**
—a daily up-dated US site with good essays on key issues.

Christian Action, Research and Education (CARE), **www.care.org.uk**
—Christian perspective on bioethical issues and much, much more.

Christian Institute, **www.christian.org.uk**
—bioethical campaigning and educating information, plus useful links.

Fellowship of Independent Evangelical Churches (FIEC),
www.fiec.org.uk/citizenship.htm
—these pages contain information of bioethical interest.

Human Fertilisation and Embryology Authority (HFEA), **www.hfea.gov.uk**
—information from the statutory body on IVF and human embryo research.

Resources

Human Genetics Commission (HGC), www.hgc.gov.uk
—news and views on genetics from the government's advisory body.

International Anti-Euthanasia Task Force, www.iaetf.org
— updates on euthanasia, assisted suicide, advance directives, etc.

LIFE, www.lifeuk.org
—press releases, facts and figures, some especially designed for students.

Nuffield Council on Bioethics, www.nuffieldfoundation.org/bioethics/index.html
—a useful site to see what the opposition is thinking.

Office for National Statistics, www.statistics.gov.uk
—search for 'abortion' and download the latest figures, and save £30.

10.5 Useful addresses
CARE, 53 Romney Street, London SW1P 3RF.

Christian Institute,
26 Jesmond Street, Newcastle upon Tyne, NE2 4PQ.

House of Commons,
London SW1A 0AA.

House of Lords,
London SW1A 0PW.

LIFE,
LIFE House, Newbold Terrace, Leamington Spa CV32 4AE.

LIFE Health Centre,
Yew Tree Lane, West Derby, Liverpool L12 9HH.

Office for National Statistics,
1 Drummond Gate, London SW1V 2QQ.

Index

Index